ALL
ISRAEL

ALL
ISRAEL

EDITED BY JOSEPHINE BACON

THE
APPLE
PRESS

There is no standard English transliteration of Hebrew words, so the reader may find place names and other Hebrew words spelled differently in this book from spellings encountered elsewhere. The transliteration used here is based on that recommended by the Academy of Jewish Languages of Haifa University, which aims at making it as easy as possible for the English-speaking reader to understand how to pronounce Hebrew and Arabic words (eg, Kalkilya and not Qalqiliyya). Where Israeli place-names have a standard English name, the English name has been used and not the modern Hebrew one (eg, Jerusalem and not Yerushalayim).

To Hanna

A QUINTET BOOK

Published by The Apple Press
6 Blundell Street
London N7 9BH

ISBN 1-85076-133-7

This book was designed and produced by
Quintet Publishing Limited
6 Blundell Street
London N7 9BH

Creative Director: Peter Bridgewater
Art Director: Ian Hunt
Designer: Pete Laws
Editors: Patricia Bayer, Sheila Buff, Judith Simons
Picture Researcher: Ruth Sonntag
Illustrator: Lorraine Harrison

Typeset in Great Britain by
Central Southern Typesetters, Eastbourne
Manufactured in Hong Kong by Regent Publishing
Services Limited
Printed in Hong Kong by Leefung-Asco Printers Limited

ACKNOWLEDGEMENTS
The author and publishers would like to thank Shmuel
Moyal, Information Counsellor at the Embassy of Israel;
the Al-Ashhab family of Jerusalem; Moshe Tamir of the
Ministry of Education and Culture; Dr Menahem Shelah
of Kibbutz Mishmar Ha-Emek; Mrs Sara and Ms Tami
Oren of Tel-Aviv; Dr and Mrs Praeger of Haifa, Dr and
Mrs Dajani of Bet-Hanina; Aloof Har-Even of the Van
Leer Institute, Jerusalem; Avraham Shinhar of the
Ministry of Agriculture; Yael Vered and Ofra Ben-
Yaakov of the Ministry of Foreign Affairs; and Mr and
Mrs Low of Cardiff for their advice and assistance in the
preparation of this book.

• Contents •

INTRODUCTION

LEFT Israel is a land of stark contrasts.
Lush valleys and arid desert combine to
create a varied landscape. Here
multicoloured wild anemones are
scattered like jewels among the lush
spring grass of the Jordan Valley
following winter rainfall.

'Therefore they shall come and sing in the height of
Zion and shall flow together . . . for wheat, for wine
and for oil . . . and their soul shall be as a watered
garden; and they shall not sorrow any more at all
. . . and there is hope in thine end . . . that thy
children shall come again to their own border.'

JEREMIAH 31:12–17

ISRAEL IS A LAND of contrast and paradox.
This tiny country, only 10,840 square miles (27,817
sq km) – roughly the size of the state of Maryland – has throughout its turbulent history occupied a position on the world stage out of all proportion to its tiny dimensions and its 4.5 million population. It is
one of the newest countries in the world, and yet one of the
oldest, whose civilization predates those of ancient Egypt and
Babylonia. Israel is a world leader in modern technology, yet a
portion of its inhabitants dress like 18th century Polish noblemen
and adhere to a strict religious code which has hardly changed
since the Middle Ages. The new cities of Israel, with their bright
neon signs, modern architecture and sidewalk cafés, resemble
those of present-day Europe; the old cities – Jerusalem, Nazareth,
Safed – are typical of the Levant.

The Israeli humorist, Ephraim Kishon, once said that there is no
point in Israel from which you could start out and drive for one
hour and not end up either in the sea or in a prisoner-of-war
camp. Despite the territorial gains of the 1967 Six Day War, this
still largely holds true. Israel is a long, narrow country (at its
southern tip, Israel is only 6 miles (9.5 km) wide). Lebanon, Syria
and Jordan, who are still officially in a state of war with Israel, are
located on the northern and eastern borders; on the western
border is Egypt, with whom the peace pact concluded in 1979 is
still rather uneasy.

The land of Israel has been the site of constant conflict for at
least five thousand years, due to its strategic position at the meeting-point of Asia and Africa, on the shores of the Mediterranean.
The conflicts have grown more frequent in modern times. The
biblical prophecy that 'in blood and fire Judaea fell and in blood
and fire Judaea will arise' has been amply fulfilled. Israel's War of
Independence actually started in 1947, when all the neighbouring
states, plus Iraq, opened hostilities before Israel could declare its
independence in 1948. Since then, the country has had to fight

three life-and-death wars, and has had to face the problem of
constant incursions of terrorists from outside, as well as from
within the territories conquered in 1967. Prior to 1967, there was
no contact between Israel and her Arab neighbours. Even now,
only contact with Egypt takes place officially.

The terrible tension of living under these conditions has left
its mark in the nervous tension displayed by many Israelis. The
native-born Israeli is called a *sabra*, the Hebrew name for the
prickly pear, because Israelis are reputed to be prickly on the
outside, but sweet inside, like the cactus fruit.

Yet the effects of Arab hostility have not all been adverse. The
Arab boycott, not only of Israeli goods but even of foreign companies trading with Israel, has forced Israel to become self-sufficient, and enabled it to produce many goods at home which

would otherwise be uneconomic due to the 'dumping' practices of some other countries. Israel is one of very few places in the Third World where you can walk into a supermarket, clothing store or gift shop, and find that almost all the goods on sale are locally made.

All these features of Israel can be found elsewhere in the world, and do not make Israel unique. What makes Israel so fundamentally different from any other country is the people. Israel is the Jewish state, the only country in the world where Judaism is the official religion, and the majority of the population is Jewish. This fact is reflected in every aspect of daily life in Israel. Saturday is the official day of rest. The Jewish Sabbath runs from dusk to dusk, so from Friday afternoon to Saturday evening there are no buses and trains, and little traffic. No shops or stores are open, no public places of entertainment (except in the West Bank and the Gaza Strip, and elsewhere in Israel itself where the majority of the population is non-Jewish). The national airline, El Al, no longer flies on the Sabbath. In hotels, hot meals are not served (it is forbidden to light fires on the Sabbath), and patrons are asked not to smoke in public.

The Jewish dietary laws are observed in all state institutions, including government offices, the Israel Defence Army, hospitals and prisons. That means no unkosher meat, no pork or shellfish, and no serving of milk and meat at the same meal.

Another consequence of being a Jewish state is that Israel is the only country in the world in which Hebrew is the official language. Hebrew, the language of the Bible, was revived over a hundred years ago as a living tongue, largely by the efforts of one man, Eliezer Ben-Yehuda (1858–1922). Hebrew has been a tremendous unifying force for the Jews who have come to Israel from every corner of the globe. Most of these Jews knew a Jewish language (Yiddish, Yavanic, Ladino, Judezmo) which may even have been written in Hebrew characters (though not necessarily using the Hebrew script current in Israel today). However, each community had its own Jewish language. Only Hebrew, the language of prayer, was common to all. For this reason, only Hebrew could be the official Jewish language. The revival of Hebrew in modern life will be discussed later in this book; but the squarish, simplified lines of Hebrew blazing out from neon signs, posters and television ads is another unique feature of Israel.

Apart from the traditional observance of Judaism (the preserve of the orthodox and ultra-orthodox, who still constitute a minority of the nation but have a disproportionate influence in society), Jewish attitudes and values prevail throughout the nation. Anthropologists such as Margaret Mead established this link

RIGHT *Harvesting red peppers in the Negev Desert. The Israelis' dedication to hard work indeed has made the desert 'blossom like the rose'. Each year, a little more of the infertile, inhospitable desert is conquered.*

FAR RIGHT *The lush plains below the Hills of Judaea are excellent vine-growing country, and have been used for this purpose since the dawn of history.*

between disparate Jewish communities long ago, before the Jews had their own country; its existence is amply demonstrated in Israel.

The two most fundamental values of Judaism are the intrinsic worth and importance of each human being, and the love of learning and scholarship. The prophets of the Old Testament did not hestitate to rebuke noblemen and kings to their faces in a way unparalleled at the time. The freedom to criticize and complain on every level continues today. Other Middle Eastern countries may hold elections, but Israel is the only true democracy. The electoral system is based on true proportional representation, which manifests itself in a multiplicity of political parties, some of which have only one member in the Knesset, Israel's parliament. The major parties represent the same left-wing and right-wing trends that one finds in other countries. Other smaller parties consist of pressure groups that strive to introduce stronger re-ligious observance into public life, to fight for the rights of Jewish and non-Jewish minorities, and to represent other factional interests. The same groupings are to be found to a more limited extent in the local government of cities, towns and settlements.

This diversity of opinion is represented in the Israeli press, which is one of the most prolific and heterogeneous in the world.

ABOVE *Baptismal site on the River Jordan. Christians of all denominations live and work in Israel, though the majority of native-born Christians are Greek Catholic.*

FAR LEFT TOP *Building a new settlement in Galilee. The pick and shovel have given way to the earthmover and bulldozer, but the pioneering spirit remains the same.*

FAR LEFT BELOW *Harvesting dates at Kibbutz Ein Gev in the Jordan Valley. This equipment is adapted from the type of crane used to maintain street-lighting!*

LEFT *Students at the Hebrew University in Jerusalem. The university is open to all, Jews and non-Jews, Israelis and non-Israelis. Many Arabs, both men and women, study at Israeli universities. There is also an Arab university at Bir Zeit on the West Bank.*

Ever since the Declaration of Independence in 1948, and up to the present time, conflict and disagreement have found their free expression in the press, radio and television, where censorship is non-existent, except in matters of security, and occasionally in immigration matters.

The strength of the press is also an expression of the literacy of the population, an aspect of the Jewish love of learning. It is not for nothing that the Jews are called the People of the Book. Not only did they produce the Bible, the Talmud and a vast collection of commentaries, interpretations and glosses unparalleled in the literature of other religions, but Jews continue to be prolific readers and writers in their own land. According to a UNESCO survey, Israelis read and publish more books per head of the population than any other people in the world. Each Israeli aged 14 and upwards reads on average one book per month.

Jewish immigration to the land they were forced to leave nearly two thousand years ago is one of the most extraordinary stories of our time. In 1947, the Jewish population of Palestine, a territory ruled by the British under a mandate granted in 1922 by the former League of Nations, was 350,000. Many of these Jews were Zionists. Named for Mount Zion, one of the hills of Jerusalem, Zionists are people who see Israel as the homeland of the Jewish people. The Zionists who arrived before the State of Israel was established, and without whom Israel would have been impossible, came as idealists, pioneers fired by visionaries in Russia and Poland and above all by Theodor Herzl, the Viennese journalist whose first encounter with anti-semitism at the Dreyfus trial in 1894 converted him to the idea of a Jewish state. Today, there are four million Jews in Israel, one million of whom arrived during the first year of statehood! The problem of taking people from all over the world, with a variety of customs, cultures and languages, and turning them virtually overnight into one nation would have proved insuperable anywhere but in Israel. Only the unifying factors of a common religion – Judaism – a national language – Hebrew – and the Jewish values described above have kept the nation together, and welded its people into ever more homogeneous nationhood as the years go by.

Of course, not all of Israel's inhabitants are Jewish. Judaism inspired the two other monotheistic religions, Christianity and Islam, and it is also a Holy Land for these religions. The place-names of Israel – Galilee, the River Jordan, Jerusalem, Tiberias – are as familiar to Christians all over the world as are the place-names in their own countries. The Mosque of Omar on Temple Mount in Jerusalem and the Tombs of the Patriarchs in Hebron are holy places for the Moslems. Israel has a large non-Jewish population; in fact, every sixth Israeli is a non-Jew, and Arabic, like Hebrew, is an official language. The Moslems of Nazareth (a predominantly Moslem city), the Christians of the village of Abu Ghosh near Jerusalem, and the Druze of Daliat-al-Carmel are equal citizens of the State of Israel, and are making their contribution to the State in the same way as its Jewish citizens. They elect Arab Knesset members (or vote for Arab members of other political parties) who may address the Knesset in Arabic, Israel's other official language.

As the years go by, the diverse cultures of the citizens of Israel are blending together. As Jews from less-developed countries marry those from Europe and the Americas, cultural differences are disappearing, and a truly Israeli lifestyle is emerging. Israel is striving to support this lifestyle, while making valiant efforts to preserve the unique Jewish folklore which the immigrants brought with them from the Diaspora (the Jewish dispersion throughout the world). The traditions of all the various strands, Jewish and non-Jewish, which go to make up Israel give Israeli life its unique flavour, a flavour which we shall do our best to convey in this book.

THE LAND OF ISRAEL

LEFT *Typical scene in the Judaean Hills, near Jerusalem, showing a new settlement cut out of the rocky ground. The vegetation consists mainly of cypress and olive trees.*

16

16

OPPOSITE LEFT *The Jordan as it winds down to the Sea of Galilee. The bare mountains of Syria contrast sharply with the rich greenery of heavily cultivated Israeli land.*

OPPOSITE TOP RIGHT *The Hazbani, one of the streams which are the sources of the River Jordan. This one is in the Golan Heights, and was Syrian territory prior to 1967. The Jordan is a very important source of water to the Israelis.*

OPPOSITE BOTTOM RIGHT *The Ta'anakh waterfall near Metulla, on the Banyas stream (a source of the River Jordan). Banyas is a corruption of the name of the god Pan to whom the Syrian-Greeks dedicated the stream. Nearby there is a shrine to the god.*

RIGHT *Papyrus growing in the Hula Lake. The Hula was once a large swamp which covered all of the Upper Galilee inland lowlands. Now it has been drained, and just a small portion of it left as a lake to preserve its unique wildlife, including the papyrus reed.*

'. . . A land of brooks of water, of fountains and depths that spring out of valleys and hills; a land of wheat and barley and vines and fig trees and pomegranates; a land of olive oil and honey; a land wherein thou shall eat bread without scarceness, thou shalt not lack any thing it it.'

DEUTERONOMY 8:7–9

THE LANDSCAPE

THE GLORY OF ISRAEL'S countryside is due in large part to the huge variety of different landscapes enclosed within its boundaries. Travelling from north to south you will first encounter the high peaks of the Golan Heights, some of which are snow-capped all year round, and pass through the green mountainous landscape of Upper Galilee, with the Hula Lake at its southern end. This lake was once much bigger and – like Israel's other inland waterways – surrounded by malarial swamps. The area has now been drained and the lake left as a nature reserve rich in a magnificent variety of wildlife. This is one of the few places where the elegant papyrus reed (from which the Egyptians first made paper) grows wild. The River Jordan is the result of the confluence of three springs, two of which, the Banyas and the Dan, are in Upper Galilee. The Jordan flows southward, through Lake Hula and into the Sea of Galilee, emerging at the other end. The 'mighty Jordan' may look far from impressive to anyone familiar with the Mississippi or even the Thames at its widest point, but it is a major waterway for the whole region, providing both Israel and Jordan with a large part of their irrigation waters.

Lack of water is a serious problem in Israel. 'We are living on borrowed water', says Avraham Shinhar from the Ministry of Agriculture. 'The water table has dropped, the water levels in the Sea of Galilee have fallen and the Jordan waters are diminishing thanks to heavy use. Water is our most vital resource and our most serious problem'. Rainfall, which is limited throughout Israel to the months between October and May, ranges from 60 inches (150 cm) on Mount Hermon in the Golan Heights, Israel's highest mountain, to less than 1 inch (25 mm) at the extreme south of the country, around Eilat.

Of all Israel's inland lakes, the Sea of Galilee (usually known in Israel as Lake Kinneret) is undoubtedly the most beautiful. Set below sea level, amidst hills dotted with outcrops of black, vol-

canic rock, the colour of the water changes with the seasons, and some people say it looks different on each day of the year. Here, at Tiberias on the lake shore, is where Jesus walked and fished, Tabgha is where he performed the multiplication of the loaves and the fishes (and the ancient church has a mosaic floor to commemorate the event), and at Capernaum he preached in the synagogue. A synagogue built on the same site in the 6th century can still be visited. It has Corinthian columns and mosaic flooring.

West of Lake Kinneret are the hills and valleys of Lower Galilee. The main city in this area is Nazareth, where Jesus' home can still be seen. Despite its Christian associations most of the inhabitants are Moslem. Nazareth is surrounded by agricultural communities, both Jewish and Arab, and nearby is the fertile Jezreel Valley, which is green all year round with intensive farming.

The Jordan continues its southward journey, through the Beth Shean Valley. Famous for its date palms, this is a hot area, below

18

LEFT *The rocky hills of Samaria are difficult to cultivate. Nevertheless, after centuries of neglect, Jewish settlers are attempting to turn these hills green again. This is a new settlement near Sebastia.*

RIGHT *Fishermen cast their nets on the Sea of Galilee, in the time-honoured way, just as Peter and his brother Andrew, John and James must have done.*

sea level, where Israel's highest temperatures have been recorded. To the west are the rounded hills of Samaria, a semi-arid region, of sparse population but great archaeological interest, since it contains the historically important town of Samaria-Sebastia.

Along the Mediterranean coast are the rounded hills of the Carmel range with Haifa at their centre. As you travel on, you come to Israel's 'waistline', where the country is only about 10 miles (16 km) wide. At this point, the 1947 United Nations partition plan divided Israel in two, because Jewish settlement in the region was so sparse. When the cease-fire lines were drawn after Israel's War of Independence (1948), part of the railroad line running north from Haifa to Jerusalem remained in Jordan. The Cease-fire Agreement of 1949 handed all of the line, and the land surrounding it, to Israel. This left the eastern side of the line within a few feet of the Jordanian border. Before the occupation of the West Bank after the Six Day War (1967), there was a joke that instead of the usual notice saying 'Don't lean out of the window', the train windows bore a sign saying 'Don't lean out of the country'! The rich, red soil and intensive farming demonstrate the fertility of this region. It is the Plain of Sharon, where the famous Rose (or Lily) of Sharon and the Sharon wild tulip can be seen growing in abundance after the spring rains.

The Plain of Sharon and the Inland Plain surrounding Ben-Gurion International Airport are important citrus-producing areas. In the summer, air travellers are greeted as they descend the plane's steps by a waft of heady perfume from the orange blossoms in the surrounding groves. In winter, there is the tangy scent of ripe Jaffa (shamouti) oranges, which glow brightly among the foliage as they wait to be picked.

20

RIGHT *Picking the crop in the citrus orchards of the Plain of Sharon.*

BELOW RIGHT *The Charles Clore International House at the Weizmann Institute, Rehovot. The Institute is surrounded by magnificent gardens and groves of mango trees.*

OPPOSITE LEFT *The remains of a mosaic floor at the palace of King Hisham with the lush green oasis of Jericho in the background, topped by the crags of the Judaean Desert.*

OPPOSITE RIGHT *Netanya, a popular seaside resort on the Mediterranean between Tel-Aviv and Haifa. In summer, the beaches of Israel are thronged with bathers, both local people and tourists.*

Travelling on south, the villages become ever more closely spaced until they finally merge into the metropolitan sprawl of Tel-Aviv, Israel's largest city. Here, the soil is sandy, and the sand dunes continue southward forming a strip as wide as 4.5 miles (7 km) past Jaffa, Tel-Aviv's twin city, to the south and along the shoreline, where one of the oldest Jewish agricultural settlements is located at Rishon-le-Zion. This colony of Jewish settlers was founded in the 1880s by immigrants from Russia, who called themselves the Bilu, an acronym formed by the initials from the biblical quotation 'House of Jacob, let us arise and go'. Nearby Rehovot is the home of the prestigious Weizmann Institute of Science, a postgraduate research institution named for the first president of the State of Israel, who was himself a scientist of note. The Institute has magnificent gardens dominated by mango trees, whose delicious fruit may be sampled if you arrive at the right time of year. There is a joke that more of the Institute's budget is spent on the greenery than on the scientists!

To the east of the coastal plain lie the semi-arid, hilly regions of Samaria and Judaea. Israel's eternal capital, Jerusalem, dominates the eastern edge of the Judaean Hills, almost overlooking the abrupt descent into the Rift Valley of the Jordan. While the northern end of the Jordan Valley, in Galilee, is relatively well-watered, rainfall is sparse in this southerly part. This fact, and the high salt concentration in the soil, have turned it into a desert. This mountainous section of the Judaean Desert contains the re-

mains of the fortress of Herodion, built by King Herod the Great. It once housed one of his magnificent palaces.

The desert swiftly drops down to the deepest part of the Rift Valley. Here, just north of the Dead Sea, there is another oasis, Jericho (in the occupied West Bank), a popular winter resort, and, according to archaeologists, probably the oldest site of continuous habitation in the world. This was a popular site for palaces; the palace of King Hisham, an early Christian monarch, stands in ruins at the northern edge of the city, and the remains of Herod's palace have also been found. The remains of the swimming pool can still be seen in which King Herod had the young Aristobulus, the rightful heir to the throne of Judaea, drowned.

The climate around Jericho is particularly suitable for tropical crops that do not grow well beside the Mediterranean, such as

THE DEAD SEA

LEFT Floating on the Dead Sea is a singular experience. The buoyancy created by the saltiest sea in the world makes one feel one is almost sitting on top of the water.

RIGHT General view over the Dead Sea, one of the most extraordinary geological phenomena in the world and the lowest point on the face of the earth. Whether or not the story of Sodom and Gomorrah is true, geologists agree that a gigantic explosion occurred on the site, creating the Rift Valley, which runs right down into Africa as far as Mount Kilimanjaro.

RIGHT Ein Gedi, a miraculous oasis in this harshest of deserts, is a magnet for all the regions wild animals, which come to drink at the waterfall when the tourists have gone. In winter, when there are fewer humans around, this is an excellent spot for bird-watching.

ABOVE These extraordinary crystalline formations that resemble stalactites form and dissolve in the shallower parts of the Dead Sea. The valuable minerals are harvested by both Israel and Jordan, since the sea is split between both countries.

24

◦ ISRAELI WILDLIFE ◦

*'I know all the fowls of the mountains and the wild
beasts of the fields are mine.'*

PSALM 50:11

ABOVE A yellow scorpion, one of the desert's less pleasant inhabitants, lives under rocks and tends to come out only when the air is cooler.

TOP An ibex poses for the camera in a Negev oasis. Most Israeli wild animals are nocturnal, less for fear of man than from a desire to escape the heat.

ABOVE Cranes outlined against a summer sunset wait for dusk until they feel safe to fly down to drink. These birds pass through Israel twice a year on their migrations. There is a theory that birds learn to avoid flying over countries in which they are heavily hunted. Israelis do not hunt for sport.

papayas and pomelos, the huge citrus fruit twice the size of grape-fruit which is becoming popular in Europe and the east coast of the United States. Jericho is dominated by a flat-topped mountain, the Mount of Temptation, where Satan is said to have tempted Jesus.

South of Jericho, the Dead Sea laps lazily along a white shore-line, whose soil consists of 90 per cent sodium chloride (common salt). The 'sea' is actually a lake – but one which is unique in the world. It has the highest concentration of salt of any stretch of water (between 28 and 33 per cent depending on the depth of the water layer). It is also the lowest point on the face of the earth, 1,300 feet (430 m) below sea level.

At the northern end of the Dead Sea lies the oasis of Ein Feshkha, where a freshwater stream feeds into the lake, and you can bathe in both fresh and briny water in turn. At almost the midway point between the northern and southern ends of the Sea, Ein Gedi, the most beautiful oasis in Israel, is hidden amid the surrounding mountains. It has a deep freshwater pool, fed by a small waterfall. Ein Gedi is one of Israel's largest nature reserves and an excellent spot for watching the wide variety of wildlife, especially birds, which come to drink.

Thanks to its geographical location at the meeting point of three continents, Israel has a huge variety of plant and animal life, including 150 plants which grow only in Israel. Some of these, such as the wild tulip, anemone, iris and cyclamen, are used by horti-culturalists to strengthen cultivated strains all over the world. All these wild flowers are protected, and can be seen at their best after the heaviest winter rains, in February and March.

The larger plants include the characteristic thorn bushes (for which the Hebrew word *shittim* is used in the King James version of the Bible), which are dotted over the desert landscape of the southern Negev. In Galilee, there are several varieties of native oak and terebinth trees. The terebinth, which confusingly is called an oak in the King James version of the Bible, is the tree whose branches hung low enough to ensnare the rebellious Absalom by the hair and trap him as he fled from his father, King David (II Samuel 18:9). The sycamore (*Ficus sicomorus*) is a native tree, whose characteristically shaped leaf, a little bit like a maple leaf, is used as the logo of the Israel Defence Force's equivalent of the American army PX (Post Exchange), or the British NAAFI. In the far south, the strange branching palm tree can be found near Eilat.

So many of Israel's native utilitarian plants have been cultivated for so long (date, fig, pomegranate, sage, thyme, marjoram) that it is hard to tell which have remained unchanged by man and which have been developed and bred for their usefulness. Certainly, as a

result of the wide range of climates and terrains, the range of flora is among the most extensive in the world – 2,300 species belonging to about 700 genera.

Many sub-tropical and desert plants from other parts of the world have been imported into Israel, where some now grow semi-wild. The most notable of these is the very plant for which the Israel-born generation of Jews is named – the sabra. Cacti are not native to the Middle East, and the prickly pear, known in Israel as the sabra, was brought from Arizona in the 19th century. Young Israelis are named for the fruit of the prickly pear because they are reputed to be prickly on the outside and sweet inside. The prickly pear is extensively used as a natural, living fence, especially by the Arabs. Strangely, it does not grow in the Israeli desert, but is found only in the central region and Lower Galilee.

There are 350 varieties of bird, 80 reptiles, 70 mammals and eight amphibians which are native to Israel. Most of the animals mentioned in the Bible can still be found in Israel, though, sadly, due to extensive hunting in the last century, the biggest mammals,

RIGHT Reboudia pinnata *cover the whole of Wadi Mashash in the northern Negev. These carpets of flowers spring up almost overnight after a wet winter.*

BELOW RIGHT *Desert broom blooming in the sand dunes. Succulents like these manage to extract moisture from the most barren soils.*

BELOW *Wild lupins (*lupinus pilosus*) growing in the hills of Galilee. The seeds of cultivated lupins are soaked in water for several days to leech out the bitterness, then salted and eaten as snacks.*

THE FLOWERS OF ISRAEL

FAR LEFT *Massed blooms in the Avdat National Park. The park has been created around the ancient archaeological site of Avdat, once a city of the Nabateans, an Arab nation which became Christian and controlled the trade routes through the Middle East in Roman times.*

LEFT *The prickly pear, or 'sabra', in bloom. All cacti were originally brought to the Middle East in the 19th century from the southwestern United States, where they flourish in a similar climate. In the foreground are native poppies.*

'Consider the lilies of the field, how they grow. They toil not, neither do they spin . . . That even Solomon in all his glory was not arrayed like one of these.'

MATTHEW 6:28, 29

such as lions, are extinct here. Occasionally, a tiger will wander into Galilee from eastern Asia, in search of the ibex and gazelles which roam Galilee, and can be glimpsed drinking at the quieter oases in the Negev. Cheetahs inhabit the Jordan Valley, and there are about 20 pairs of leopards, who are nocturnal thanks to the intense heat, in an area near the Dead Sea. Wild boar are still to be found in Galilee, though unfortunately they are hunted since they tend to dig up and eat the crops at night. Jackals and foxes are also exterminated outside the national parks, because their liking for chickens makes them unwelcome visitors to farms. There are a few wild camels in the southern Negev, but these animals were domesticated so many thousands of years ago no one is sure if they are native to Israel or not.

While some animals are becoming rarer due to urban development, and pesticides have affected the number of birds of prey, such as the raven, griffon-vulture and serpent eagle, which are mentioned in the Bible, other birds are actually becoming more numerous. This is thanks to the greater water resources available to them from Israel's ever-extending agriculture, and the fish farmed in ponds. Thus, the heron, cormorant and water-loving animals like the marsh-lynx are on the increase, to say nothing of the multitude of frogs, whose nightly croaking round ponds and swimming pools is almost deafening! The bulbul, another bird mentioned in the Bible, is becoming a pest because it loves to eat flowerbuds and Israel has a flourishing flower-exporting industry. Many varieties of bird pass through Israel on their migratory route from Europe to Africa, and so are not counted as native species.

There are many snakes in Israel, of which some are harmless, like the black snake and the sand boa. The most dangerous is the Palestinian viper, but like most snakes it prefers to avoid humans. Millipedes and particularly the several varieties of scorpion cause more casualties, and for this reason people are advised not to wear sandals when hiking off the road in the Negev.

The best time and place to see wildlife is at dusk or dawn near waterholes or man-made sprinkler systems.

Israel has an active Nature Reserves Authority, established in 1964, and for such a tiny country is an amazing number of nature reserves, 280 at the time of writing, covering nearly 400,000 acres (161,872 hectares). Israelis take an enormous pride in the wildlife of the country, and from an early age children know they are forbidden to pick the wild flowers or disturb wild animals. There is hardly any game hunting in Israel, in contrast to the rest of the Mediterranean region.

South of Ein Gedi stands another mountain fortress built by Herod, that of Masada, where a gallant band of 1,000 Jews – men, women and children – held out for three years against the Roman invaders, finally committing mass suicide in AD 73. Masada has become a place of pilgrimage for modern Israelis, to remind them of how much their Jewish predecessors sacrificed for their country.

The small settlement of Sodom stands on the southern shore of the Dead Sea. Far from looking like the den of vice described in the Bible, and which God destroyed, the new Sodom is mainly a health spa, where the Dead Sea mud bath cure is said to be effective against rheumatism and skin diseases (Gomorrah has vanished entirely into the waters!). The local minerals are also incorporated into Israeli skin creams and mud packs, but the most profitable use of the Dead Sea minerals is at the nearby Dead Sea Works, where potash, nitrates and bitumen are extracted. The Dead Sea is a pleasant place to visit in winter, but in summertime temperatures can reach 122°F (50°C)! Behind Sodom is the strangely shaped Mount Sodom, a mountain of salt and gypsum, rising over 600 feet (200 m) above the level of the waters, which is also referred to as 'Lot's Wife' (who was changed into a pillar of salt; Gen 19:26).

BELOW A *happy, mud-covered bather at the Ein Bokek resort on the Dead Sea. The mud is said to cure rheumatism and be extremely effective in combating skin diseases such as psoriasis and sebhorraeic dermatitis.*

THE NEGEV IN WINTER

RIGHT *Vines growing in the Lachish area inland from the Gaza Strip. This area, once the heart of Philistea, the land inhabited by the Philistines, and consequently rich in archaeological remains, is a fertile, agricultural area. Nearby is Heletz; where oil was first discovered in Israel.*

ABOVE *Tomatoes being grown hydroponically at Ben-Gurion University in the Negev, part of Kibbutz Sde Boker, where David Ben-Gurion, Israel's first prime minister, made his home towards the end of his life.*

The River Jordan flows into the Dead Sea at its northern end, but because the Jordan waters are so heavily exploited for irrigation purposes, the level of the Dead Sea is dropping rapidly. For this reason, a Mediterranean–Dead Sea canal has been mooted. This 65-mile (104 km) stretch of waterway would have to drop sharply to reach the Dead Sea 1,000 feet (300 m) below the level of the Mediterranean. The artificial waterfall which would thus be created could power a hydroelectric scheme, a valuable potential addition to Israel's enormous power needs. As a highly industrialized country, Israel is the biggest consumer of energy in the region, yet it has few natural energy resources of its own.

West of the Dead Sea, at Israel's widest point the Coastal Plain stretches past Israel's second-largest port, Ashdod, to the Gaza Strip where it meets the desert of the Sinai Peninsula. Inland, the fertile but dry Judaean Plain becomes more and more devoid of vegetation until it evolves into a succession of sand dunes, the northern part of the Negev Desert. The capital city of this region is Beer-Sheba, which still has the atmosphere of a frontier town. Many of Beer-Sheba's residents are Jewish immigrants from North Africa and Iraq. The town is surrounded by agricultural settlements whose occupants come from a wide variety of backgrounds, including one moshav (cooperative village) whose residents are Jews from Cochin, India. On market days, the local Bedouin Arabs come into town with their camels to buy and sell.

RIGHT The Wilderness of Zin in the northern Negev, a rocky landscape dotted with thorn bushes, where Bedouins graze their flocks, watering them at the few oases.

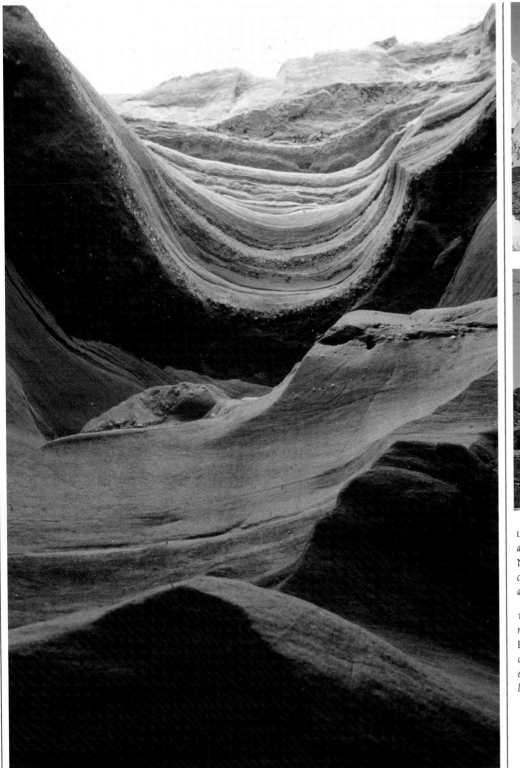

LEFT These strange formations of rocks and sand dunes are frequently seen in the Negev Desert. They are caused by a combination of ancient volcanic activity and subsequent erosion.

TOP Typical of the Arava are these rocky crags near the Egyptian border. Fossilized sea shells can be found on top of them, an indication that before the explosion that occurred at Sodom, they lay at the bottom of a shallow sea.

ABOVE The Pillars of Solomon, near the copper mines of Timnah, about 45 minutes drive north of Eilat at the southern tip of Israel. The copper mines are among the oldest continuously worked mines in the world; copper is still being extracted from them. There has been mining activity in the area since prehistoric times, long before the reign of King Solomon.

The main road south through the Negev becomes ever more barren, until it reaches a huge escarpment called the Makhtesh Ramon. There are two other similar rock formations, the Makhtesh Ha-Gadol (Large Crater) and the Makhtesh Ha-Katan (Small Crater) to the west of it. All are outcrops of volcanic rock, set in a landscape so rugged and barren that it resembles a moonscape. The cliff of the Makhtesh Ramon, which looks like a miniature Grand Canyon, forms the border between the northern and southern parts of the Negev. The southern Negev is also called the Arava Desert. The Arava is a dry, sandy valley between two ranges of mountains. What little vegetation there is consists of sparse thorn and acacia trees and the land is so salty that it is an effort to make things grow. However, agricultural research, at which the Israelis are world leaders, has established that some crops grow well in brackish water, and the agricultural settlements that have been established in the Arava are thriving. Tomatoes, for instance, turn the salt in the soil into sugar, making the fruits taste almost as sweet as candy.

The Arava stretches southward between two high mountain ranges. To the east are the Mountains of Edom, which lie in Transjordan. The word *edom* means red, and they are indeed red sandstone mountains, at the heart of which stands the abandoned city of Petra, 'the rose red city half as old as time', still, unfortunately, out of bounds to Israeli visitors. To the west are the Negev Highlands, a continuation of the mountains of the Sinai Peninsula, whose most famous peak is, of course, Mount Sinai, where Moses is supposed to have received the Tablets of the Law. The monastery of Saint Catherine on the mountain slopes, now in Egypt, is accessible by day excursion from Israel.

At the southern tip of the Arava are some spectacular geological formations, sandstone columns known as the Pillars of Solomon. They lie near Timnah, a copper mine that has been exploited since prehistoric times. This is the genuine site of King Solomon's mines (the ones in the book by H Rider Haggard were relocated by the author to southern Africa). Copper is still being extracted five thousand years later. A park, containing a grove of trees and an artificial lake, is being built at Timnah. This not only adds interest to the area, but as experiments have shown, newly created expanses of water in arid regions encourage natural precipitation, thus bringing in much-needed natural water.

The Negev provides Israel's flourishing jewellery industry with many semi-precious stones. Many quartz-based gemstones are to be found in the Negev, but the most popular souvenir jewellery is made from Eilat stone, a turquoise-coloured by-product of the copper-rich rock, similar to malachite.

LEFT *Diving among the beautiful corals and tropical fish of the Red Sea. Strenuous efforts are made to protect this unique marine environment from the depradations of tourists, and it is strictly forbidden to pick any corals.*

RIGHT *Tel-Aviv, looking along the promenade towards the big seafront hotels.*

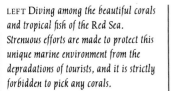

ABOVE *These stamps feature a selection of the magnificent tropical fish commonly found in the coral reefs off Eilat in the Red Sea. From top to bottom are the angel fish, the butterfly fish, the fire fish, whose spines are poisonous, and the pennant coral fish. For those who are not energetic enough to go scuba diving and see the fish in their natural surroundings, Eilat has a very well-appointed museum of marine life.*

The Red Sea port of Eilat, at the southernmost tip of the desert, is the major population centre. The Negev Desert is triangular in shape, and Eilat forms the apex of this triangle; at this point, Israel is only 6 miles (9.6 km) wide. Eilat has grown from a few wooden huts in 1956, to a Wild-West-style frontier town in 1967, to today's smart tourist resort where luxury hotels jockey for position along the sandy shoreline and there are direct winter sunshine charter flights from northern Europe. Eilat has plenty of water sports including waterskiing, and especially scuba diving. The Red Sea is very shallow (by marine standards) and full of corals which encourage a wide variety of beautiful tropical fish. For the less active, marine life can also be seen through glass-bottomed boats and in the local museum.

THE CITIES OF ISRAEL

More than 85 per cent of Israelis live in cities. Some are on sites which have been inhabited for thousands of years, such as the cities of Tiberias and Safed in Galilee and Hebron (in the occupied West Bank), all of which are holy to the Jews, as well as Nazareth, and Acre and Jaffa on the coast. There are the new 'development towns' founded in the 1950s and 1960s to cope with the vast influx of Jewish immigration, first from war-torn Europe, then from North Africa and the Arab world. These include Kiryat Shemona and Carmiel in Upper Galilee and Dimona and Kiryat Gat in the northern Negev. The major port of Ashdod and the nearby resort city of Ashkelon are also new towns, which, like Kiryat Gat, are in that part of the coastal plain once inhabited by the Philistines. Gath was famous as Goliath's home town. ('Tell it not in Gath, publish it not in the streets of Ashkelon'; II Samuel 2:10). All Israeli cities, old and new, planned and unplanned, are liberally supplied with parks and recreation areas.

JERUSALEM The Eternal City, Israel's capital, has a population of less than half a million. So much has been written and said about Jerusalem, and there is so much to say, that it would take a book far longer than this one just to give a bare glimpse of the city's attractions.

One of the most spectacular aspects of Jerusalem is its setting, high amongst the beehive-shaped, rocky Hills of Judaea. From whichever direction you approach Jerusalem, you have to climb up to it. The main road from the west, that is, from Tel-Aviv, Haifa and Ben-Gurion International Airport, winds from the coastal plain up through the low foothills. At the monastery of Latrun, the road forks. The northern fork goes up to Ramallah, the southern to Jerusalem. This part of the road was in Jordanian hands

RIGHT A Street in Jerusalem, *by the artist Jakob Steinhardt, best known for his woodcuts. This work was produced in 1934, but the old quarters of Jerusalem, both inside and outside the Old City walls, still look like this, but for the addition of a forest of tall television aerials on the roofs.*

ABOVE *General view of the Old City of Jerusalem, looking eastward. The golden dome is the Mosque of Omar, set on Temple Mount. The mosque contains the Even Ha-Shetiyah, the stone which Jews believe is the foundation stone of the Temple and of the world, and the site on which Abraham laid Isaac to sacrifice him. Moslems believe that it was from here that Mohammed ascended to heaven on his horse, Al-Buraq, which left a hoofprint in the rock.*

until 1967, and an alternative, southern route was cut from the rock. As the road climbs through the Sha'ar Ha-Gai (Bab El-Wad), the Gateway to the Pass, the remains of trucks and armoured vehicles, carefully painted to preserve them against rust, lie on either side of the road. They are a memorial to those who died in the convoys, trying to keep the road open during Israel's War of Independence. The stretch of road which had to be built to link the sections in Israeli hands and bypass that which was held by the Jordanians was completed in record time, by volunteers working day and night, and was known as 'The Burma Road', in memory of the road which was built by British, American and Chinese forces to link the Burma/Assam front with China.

Finally, at the steepest part of the climb, the hilltops are no longer bare but are covered with houses – the outskirts of Jerusalem. The new city, built by Israelis, has spread westward, because before 1967 Jerusalem was surrounded by a hostile border on

three sides. The newest suburbs stretch towards the lonely mosque of Nebi Musa and the outskirts of the city of Ramallah. They encompass the Sanhedriya, the tombs built by Jewish noblemen in the early centuries of the Christian era. The Old City is still out of sight at this point.

The classic camera view of the Old City of Jerusalem is from the Mount of Olives, which lies on its eastern side. From here you can see in the city wall built by Suleiman the Magnificent in the 16th century, a gate that has been walled up. This is the so-called Golden Gate; Jews claim that it will open only for the Messiah.

The Mount of Olives is the largest Jewish graveyard in Israel. It is to the Mount of Olives that all Jewish souls are traditionally supposed to 'roll' in the Last Days, so being buried on the Mount of Olives means being among the first in line at the Day of Judgement. Also on the Mount of Olives are two churches. High on the Mount is the Church of St Mary Magdalene, an architectural gem

with its seven glittering golden domes, owned by the Russian Orthodox Church in exile, based in the United States. The church was built by Alexander III in 1888, in memory of his mother, Maria Alexandrovna, Princess of Hesse. The Grand Duchess Elizabeth (1864-1918), sister of Alexandra, the last Czarina, is buried here. The icons inside the church, painted by Vereshaguine and Ivanoff, are well worth seeing. Directly below it, in the garden of Gethsemane, is the Church of All Nations, a gaudy monstrosity started in 1919. The name comes from the fact that many nations contributed to the work. The church is Italian and Roman Catholic. Opposite, rising above the city walls (and the host of television aerials on the houses inside them) are a large golden dome and a smaller silver one. The golden dome belongs to the Mosque of the Dome of the Rock, one of Islam's holy sites. The dome covers a huge rock from which the Moslems allege that Mohammed ascended into heaven on his horse, Al-Buraq. The hoofprint is said to be visible in the rock. The Jews believe that this stone, which they call *Even Ha-Shetiyah* (the Foundation Stone), was originally the stone on which Abraham laid Isaac to be sacrificed, and became the foundation stone of the Temple.

If you enter the Old City from the Lion Gate (also known as St Stephen's Gate), the nearest gate to the Dome, you can see that the whole area is built up on a platform, the so-called Temple Mount. The Dome of the Rock stands in a large courtyard. Opposite, the silver-domed building is the Mosque of Al-Aqsa, the most important Moslem place of worship in the city. Below the Mount on the western side is the Western Wall (or Wailing Wall, as it used to be known). Although Judaism generally rejects the concept of holy places, this is the most sacred of all Jewish sites, the original wall of the Second Temple, destroyed by the Romans in AD 70. The area in front of the wall was cleared of houses in 1968 and now forms a large concourse. A barrier has been set up at the wall for men and women to pray separately.

Although the view from the Mount of Olives is spectacular, there are two other routes into the Old City which are not so grandiose but in their way are beautiful, especially if you are on foot. If you walk from the rather ugly, rundown commercial centre of western Jerusalem, along Jaffa Road, which was the main boulevard prior to 1967, when the two halves of the city were reunited, and turn up Heleni Ha-malka (Queen Helen) Street, you will pass the Israel Radio station on your left, while on your right is the Russian Compound, dominated by the green-domed Russian Orthodox Church. This church belongs to the Church in the Soviet Union, though the compound itself, a walled enclosure containing outbuildings, has been purchased by the State of Israel and houses a lot of government offices. The church can be visited. You continue down the narrow street, past the point which was once no man's land, blocked off by fire walls with gun-slits in

ABOVE LEFT *Jerusalem. A view of the Citadel of David and the western side of the 16th-century city wall built by Suleiman the Magnificent to keep out the Crusaders.*

ABOVE *The Mount of Olives, seen through one of the arches on Temple Mount known as King Solomon's Stables. The Mount of Olives contains the most important Jewish graveyard in the world, as well as several churches. On top is the steeple of a French church.*

THE GATES OF JERUSALEM

LEFT Herod's Gate, one of the entrances to Temple Mount, overlooked by the silver dome of the Mosque of El-Aqsa, one of Islam's holiest shrines. Herod refurbished the Second Temple, the only tangible example of his identification with his fellow Jews, but this did nothing to endear him to his people.

BELOW LEFT The New Gate, seen from inside the Old City. This gate faces the western side of the city and was the scene of fierce fighting in Israel's War of Independence in 1948.

BELOW The Jaffa Gate seen from one side. On the other side a large gap has been made in the wall. This was produced especially for Kaiser Wilhelm II, who was able to parade on horseback through the Old City during his visit to this part of the Ottoman Empire in 1913. In 1917, General Allenby led the British and Allied troops through it on a victory march.

them, though you would never know it today since all traces have disappeared. The road suddenly widens and to your left and right are empty lots, while in front of you rises the wall of the Old City overlooking the hustle and bustle of one of the two main gates to the city, the Damascus Gate (the other is the Jaffa Gate). Arab peasant women in picturesque white veils and hand-embroidered dresses jostle with soberly dressed Arab townswomen, orthodox Jews wearing tiny knitted skullcaps confer with ultra-orthodox Hassidic Jews whose strange black garments are in the style worn by 18th-century Polish noblemen. There are ultra-orthodox Jewish women, their heads covered by wigs and scarves, and ultra-ortho-dox Moslem women wearing a grey or drab brown scarf with a shapeless robe to match (the veil covering the face is hardly ever seen in Israel). Just inside the Damascus Gate is the *souq*, the Arab market. A large part of the Old City consists of a huge market, and each street originally had its own trade. Even today, butchers, shoe shops and quiltmakers all tend to herd together.

The Old City is still divided into quarters for each of the communities which inhabit it. The Jewish quarter was destroyed after the War of Independence when the Jews were evacuated, but has now been rebuilt. There are the Moslem and Christian quarters, the latter being mainly Greek Catholic (Israel's largest Christian community), and there is an Armenian quarter, domi-nated by the magnificent Armenian church and monastery of St James the Lesser.

Another interesting route in the Old City, especially in spring, when the grass is green and full of flowers, is to climb Mount Zion, visiting David's Tomb on the way. It is supposed to be the tomb of King David, but archaeologists and historians have strong reser-vations about this. At the top of Mount Zion is the Church of the Dormition, where the Virgin Mary is supposed to have been taken up to heaven. Just over the other side of the hill is the modern but attractive church of St Peter in Gallicantu, built in 1931 on the site where St Peter is said to have heard the cock crow twice during the trial of Jesus ('Before the cock crows twice thou shalt deny me thrice'; Mark 14:72). The path leads on through green fields to either the Zim Gate or the the Dung Gate, the only gate through which ultra-orthodox Jews are allowed to enter the city, and almost immediately, you are at the Western Wall.

Jerusalem is a microcosm of Israel as a whole, an amazing mix of races and communities, of the incredibly old and the brand new. It is the home of the Knesset (Israel's parliament), the Israel Museum and the Hebrew University. It is a shrine, a seat of learn-ing and a holy city for three religions and one of the most import-ant sites in the history of the world.

• ACRE – THE CRUSADER CITY •

ABOVE In the old town of Acre (Akko), in Galilee, looking towards the Al-Jazzar Mosque, one of the most important mosques in the Holy Land. Acre, founded by the Crusaders in the 12th century, is still largely an Arab city.

RIGHT The port of Acre (Akko) is still a small fishing port, where magnificent shellfish are caught. Nearby are many good fish restaurants.

LEFT *Haifa, looking out to sea from the top of Mount Carmel. Haifa is the most European-looking of Israel's cities, and by far the cleanest. The wide boulevards are reminiscent of Switzerland, as is the mountain vegetation of pines, though these are a sub-tropical variety.*

BELOW *The most famous and notable landmark in Haifa is the Baha'i Temple. The Baha'i faith was founded in Persia (now Iran) in the 18th century, by a Persian mystic known as the Baha'ullah. Its adherents are now scattered and are persecuted in their native land, but many come here to pray and study in this magnificent temple and the adjacent library and archive. The buildings are surrounded by formal gardens of cypress and box hedges.*

HAIFA Haifa is set in a landscape no less picturesque than that of Jerusalem, but instead of nestling amid the hills, Haifa sits astride the highest hill and sweeps down to the sea. The city straddles Mount Carmel and dominates a wide bay, making it an important natural harbour. It used to be Israel's major commercial port, but it now shares importance with Ashdod, though it is still the biggest naval base, and a regular port of call for the American Sixth Fleet.

Of all the cities of Israel, Haifa is probably the most cosmopolitan in a non-Jewish sense. It has many missions and recreation facilities for foreign seamen, and there is a considerable non-Jewish population, both Christian and Moslem. It is also the spiritual centre and site of the shrine of the Baha'i faith. The beautiful Baha'i Temple and meeting place, set in elegant, formal gardens dotted with cypress trees, are an added attraction for the city. Haifa University has many non-Jewish students. The city's population is only half that of Jerusalem.

Just as the character of Jerusalem is overwhelmingly religious, Haifa's character – and population – are overwhelmingly secular.

You might have trouble finding a kosher restaurant in Haifa, where the latest craze is for Chinese food, and Chinese restaurants looking like fake pagodas are springing up all over the city! The city has a very northern European atmosphere, both in the wide avenues and the cleanliness of the streets. In fact, it is hard to believe you are in the Middle East. Only down by the port, in the old neighbourhood of Wadi Salib, does it look, sound and smell like the Mediterranean again.

The view over the bay is so magnificent that Haifa can be classed, like San Francisco, as one of the world's most beautiful ports.

TEL-AVIV Before the State of Israel was established in 1948, Tel-Aviv was regarded by Zionists all over the world and by the rest of the Jewish population of Israel as a minor miracle in its own right – the only Jewish city in the world. The name derives from the word for an old mound or site, *Tel*, and the word for spring, *Aviv*, to signify newness and rebirth. It is the name coined for the city of which Theodor Herzl, the founder of Zionism, dreamed in his book about a Jewish state, *Altneuland (Oldnewland)*.

The city was founded in 1909 as a suburb of the then main port of Jaffa. Then an Arab city, Jaffa is mentioned in texts as early as 1500 BC. Tel Aviv grew along the seashore and is constructed like a seaside resort in Europe, with a promenade (boardwalk) beside the Mediterranean. The architecture in the older streets such as Ha-Yarkon Street, A D Gordon Street, and parts of Rothschild Boulevard and Chen Boulevard is typical of German, Austrian and Czech architecture of the 1920s and 1930s. Indeed, it was the refugees from persecution in Europe who gave Tel-Aviv its architectural and cultural character, founding the Opera, the Ha-Bimah Theatre and the Israel Philharmonic Orchestra.

Tel-Aviv is still the cultural centre of the nation. It is the home of Israeli theatre and music of all types, from pop to classical. This is the home of the famous Mann Auditorium and the Cameri Theatre. The fashionable Dizengoff Square and Dizengoff Street are as full of smart boutiques as London, Paris or New York, though department stores are few (the Shalom Stores in the Shalom Tower is about the only one). Tel-Aviv is the life and soul of Israel. Its character is vivacious and energetic, in contrast to the sanctity of Jerusalem and the relative staidness of Haifa. It is the hub of business and commercial activity and the hub of pleasure. Greater Tel-Aviv includes many outlying suburbs and small towns and has grown to an urban sprawl of 1,300,000, by far the biggest metropolis in Israel.

Undoubtedly, the most striking feature of the Israeli landscape is the constant change. Anyone who saw Palestine as it was before Israel declared independence, would find many parts of the country unrecognizable. Not only have towns and villages sprung up on rocky outcrops, bare mountains and barren deserts, the countryside itself has been transformed from marsh and wilderness to flourishing agricultural land. This has been achieved at the cost of much hard work, and even of lives, through the unique Israeli network of cooperative farming communities. In the following chapters, we shall see what kind of people inhabit the cities, towns, villages and farms of Israel.

BELOW *General view of Tel-Aviv, Israel's largest metropolis. Today, more than 85 per cent of the population of Israel is city-dwelling.*

ISRAEL'S GEOGRAPHY AT A GLANCE

NAMES: Israel, Eretz-Israel (literally 'the Land of Israel'), meaning all the areas within and outside the borders which were historically settled by Israelites and Jews. Also known poetically as Zion, after the hill on which Jerusalem was first established, as The Promised Land because God promised it to Abraham, and as the Holy Land.

LOCATION: At meeting-point of Europe, Asia and Africa.

SIZE: Area: 10,840 square miles (27,817 sq km). Length: 263 miles (420 km). Width at widest point: 110 miles (160 km). Width at narrowest point: 6 miles (9.6 km).

CAPITAL: Jerusalem (pop 428,700).

MAJOR CITIES: Tel-Aviv – Jaffa (pop 327,300; Greater Tel-Aviv – Jaffa has a population of 1,300,000); Haifa (pop 225,800); Beer-Sheba (pop 110,800).

PORTS: Haifa (pop 225,800); Ashdod (pop 65,700); Eilat (pop 18,900); Hadera (pop 38,700).

SEAS: Mediterranean; Red Sea; Dead Sea; Sea of Galilee (also known as Lake Kinneret and Genasareth).

RIVERS: Jordan River, 127 miles (203 km) long, covering a distance of 186 miles (298 km); Yarkon River; all other rivers are dry for part of the year.

HIGHEST MOUNTAIN: Mount Hermon, 9,220 ft (3,073 m).

LOWEST SURFACE POINT: Sodom, the lowest place on the face of the earth.

ANNUAL RAINFALL: 1.5 in (6 mm) in the Negev Desert to 32 in (80 cm) in the Golan Heights. Rain falls only between September and May.

ANNUAL MEAN TEMPERATURES: Central plain 68°–70°F (20°–21°C); Jerusalem 65°–68°F (17°–18°C); Sea of Galilee 72.1°F (22.3°C); Dead Sea 78.3°F (25.7°C).

HIGHEST TEMPERATURE RECORDED: 131°F (54°C), in Beth Shean Valley.

LOWEST TEMPERATURE RECORDED: 19.4°F (−7°C), in Jerusalem.

THE JEWS
OF ISRAEL

LEFT This huge gathering at the Western
Wall marked the closing day of the four-day
World Meeting of Holocaust Survivors, held
in Jerusalem in June 1981. The Holocaust
affected Jews from almost every community
and changed the demographic pattern of
Jewish life throughout the world forever.

> 'For there shall be a day, that the watchmen upon
> Mount Ephraim shall cry, Arise ye, and let us go
> up to Zion . . . Behold I will bring them from the
> north country, and gather them from the coasts of
> the earth . . . a great company shall return thither.'
>
> JEREMIAH 31:6–8

WHO ARE THE JEWS?

ISRAEL IS FIRST and foremost the Jewish state, the only country in the world with a mainly Jewish population, whose official religion is Judaism. At the time of writing, the population of Israel numbers 4,106,100, of whom 82.9 per cent are Jews. Yet 100 years ago, the Jewish population of what was then Palestine numbered a few thousands, and 100 years before that, a few hundreds. The story of the resettlement of the Jews in the land which had historically been theirs for thousands of years is one of the miracles of this day and age.

Historians and archaeologists believe that a western Semitic tribe known as the Amurru (Amorites), one of the group of tribes known collectively as the Canaanites, were the first inhabitants of that part of the eastern Mediterranean, consequently known as Canaan. They apparently lived in Canaan until around 3000 BC, when they were conquered by Indo-Aryan peoples, the Hittites and the Mitani, who became rulers of the various city-states, notably Jaffa, Gaza and Arad. The Hittites are commemorated in a place-name, a strange mountain formation in Galilee known as the Horns of Hittin.

The Hittites and the Mitani were in turn driven out by the Israelites themselves, in about 1200 BC. The Israelites almost certainly arrived from the east, and it is quite probable that they came from Ur of the Chaldes (in Mesopotamia, between the Tigris and the Euphrates rivers), the birthplace of Abraham.

The nomadic Israelites eventually moved on to Egypt to escape a famine in their own land, leaving to go north again (the Exodus from Egypt) in about 1200 BC. About 100 years prior to this event, the Egyptian pharaoh, Akhnaton, had introduced significant religious reforms, involving a version of monotheism. Many historians believe that Akhnaton's beliefs did not die with him but were carried on by this northwestern Semitic immigrant tribe, the Israelites, who took them back to their own land. This was the origin of Judaism.

RIGHT *An ancient olive-press at Kursi. Olives were crushed in this way in earliest times, and the name Gethsemane indicates that there was an olive-press in the garden where Jesus spent his last hours before imprisonment.*

OPPOSITE TOP *One of the oldest archaeological sites in Israel, Tel Hazor, contains Canaanite and pre-Canaanite remains as well as relics of the Philistines.*

OPPOSITE BOTTOM *King Solomon's Pool at Siloam, near Hebron. In the 10th century BC, the kingdom of Israel was at the height of its glory, the Philistines had been defeated and Solomon, the mighty and famous monarch, had built a Temple in Jerusalem.*

The Bible records that when the Israelites returned to their land, they had to fight many battles to re-establish themselves. The Amorites were systematically wiped out, due to what the courts of law would today call 'irreconcilable differences', but other Canaanite tribes, including the Phoenicians, were gradually assimilated into the Israelite nation.

The Israelites settled in the northern and eastern parts of modern Israel, as well as some areas now on the east bank of the Jordan, but the Philistines invaded during the same period, occupying the coastal plain to the south, in what is today the Gaza Strip and inland from that point. The Philistines, who are characterized in the Bible as monsters and barbarians, came either from Crete or Cyprus, and their remains in those countries show they were very far from being uncivilized. It was merely that their culture was totally alien to the local Semitic tribes, of which the Israelites were one.

This period saw the flowering of the Kingdom of Israel, the reigns of Saul and Solomon, the final defeat of the Philistines, and the building of the Temple in Jerusalem.

After the death of King David, Israel split into two kingdoms, Israel and Judah. This weakened the Israelites considerably, and in 722 BC, the Kingdom of Israel was conquered by the Assyrians and

its people scattered forever. These came to be known as the Lost Tribes. Judah was conquered by Babylonia in 586 BC, and its people, the two remaining tribes of Israelites, Judah and Benjamin, taken away into captivity in Babylonia. There they stayed until 539 BC, lamenting their fate, and praying for the return to Zion.

The Jews, as they had now become known, only returned from Babylonia to Judaea when Babylonia was conquered by the Persians in 538 BC. The Persians were Zoroastrians, a religion which has elements of monotheism, and their king, Cyrus, felt the Jews could be valuable allies if they were restored to their ancient homeland. The walls of Jerusalem and the Temple were rebuilt, and this was a second period of glory for the nation.

However, when the Persian empire fell and the province of Jehud, as the Persians dubbed it, lost its protection, there followed successive conquests, from the relatively tolerant rule of the Ptolemies of Egypt to that of the despotic Seleucid monarch, Antiochus IV Epiphanes. The Seleucids (Syrians who had adopted the Greek religion) were finally overthrown by the Revolt of the Maccabeans in 166 BC, led by the Jewish general, Judah the Maccabee.

The Maccabees established a royal house of priest-kings, the Hasmoneans, who ruled until well into Roman times. However, the kingdom was eventually again weakened by internal strife in the royal house, and Judaea was conquered by the Romans in 37 BC. Though at first Roman rule was tolerant, treating Judaea as a vassal state, it grew ever harsher, as the Roman emperors became increasingly irked by a religion such as Judaism, which precluded its adherents from worshipping the Roman emperors as gods. Like their predecessors, the Romans considered the Jews to be an aberration, a nation with a religion so powerful it could defy the might of Rome. They finally sacked the Temple in AD 70, invading the Holy of Holies, into which only the High Priest was allowed on one day of the year. The Temple was never to be rebuilt. A group of Jews held out against the Romans in the fortress of Masada until AD 73, committing mass suicide rather than surrender.

From now on, Judaea was ruled directly from Rome, through the governors of neighbouring provinces such as Syria. Jerusalem was razed to the ground and renamed Aelia Capitolina; Jews were forbidden to live there. The whole country was given the Roman name of Palaestina, after the Philistines, the Jews' ancient enemies. For this reason, the very name 'Palestine' has disturbing associations for Jews.

Though later Roman emperors, notably Septimus Severus and his direct descendants (5th century), were more tolerant towards the remnants of the Jewish community in Israel, in general the

The Fortress of Masada is to all Israelis the ultimate symbol of Jewish courage and resistance to persecution. It was in this fortress in the Judaean Desert, originally built by Herod the Great in about 25 BC that a brave group of men, women and children held out for two years against the Romans after the destruction of the Temple in Jerusalem in AD 70. When they saw that they were about to be overwhelmed, they committed suicide. Today, a visit to Masada is part of the induction into the Israel Defence Army, and a highlight of any visit to the Negev. The view over the Dead Sea from the top of the fortress is magnificent, especially at dawn.

● THE FORTRESS OF MASADA ●

RIGHT A Persian Jew studying the Bible. The Jews have been in Persia (Iran) for as long as they have been in Iraq (Babylonia), and were deeply integrated into the community, though many were forced to practise their religion in secret, especially in the cities that were holy to Moslems, such as Meshhed. Only since the Shah of Iran was deposed have they been persecuted and forced to leave.

Jews became subject to greater and greater persecutions, particularly after Rome became Christian under Constantine the Great, in AD 318.

Gradually, the Jewish community in Palestine dwindled away. Restrictions on the practice of the Jewish religion and other forms of discrimination forced those who had not been murdered to emigrate, and by the time of the Moslem conquest of AD 637, Jews constituted only 10 per cent of the population. They continued to dwindle thereafter. Shortly after the establishment of the State of Israel in 1948, it was discovered that one large Jewish family had, in fact, remained for the entire 1,500 years in the remote Galilean village of Peki'in. This family still lives in Israel.

The Jewish dispersal, known as the Diaspora, had begun in the time of the Babylonian Exile (many Iraqi Jews proudly claim their families never left Babylonia to return to Judah). By the time of Christ, there were more Jews living outside the land of Israel than in it, including the important communities of Alexandria in Egypt and of Rome itself. So the Jews had important centres abroad which enabled their traditions and culture to survive through the ages. Even today, Israeli Jews constitute only 26.4 per cent of world Jewry. Yet no Jew ever forgets his or her spiritual homeland. At every morning, afternoon and evening service, and at every grace after meals, there are prayers recalling the Temple and Jerusalem, saying 'May He in His Mercy rebuild Jerusalem. Amen'. The song 'Ha-Tikvah' ('The Hope'), written in Poland 100 years ago, which has become the national anthem of Israel, says 'As long as there is hope in his heart, the Jew looks towards Zion'.

Jews began drifting back to the land of their forefathers from the Middle Ages onwards, to make the pilgrimage to Jerusalem and weep at the Wailing Wall (now called the Western Wall) of the Temple, almost the only part that has survived (in fact, part of the southern wall can also still be seen today). Some settled and continued to study in the cities of Safed, Hebron and Tiberias, where religious academies had flourished in the 1st and 2nd centuries AD. Yet it was not until the 19th century that a movement grew up among the persecuted masses of eastern European Jewry for a return to Zion – the movement which came to be known as Zionism.

Zionism was never a religious movement, but one whose roots were largely secular and which drew its inspiration from the national liberation movements of other minorities in the vast Austro-Hungarian and Russian empires. One of the earliest Zionist groups was known as Hovevei Zion (Lovers of Zion) or Hibbat Zion (Love of Zion). Perhaps the first written suggestion that Jews might find a refuge from the terrible persecutions they had endured throughout the centuries in the Diaspora came from Moses Montefiore, a wealthy British Jew, writing in 1838. Moses Montefiore visited the Holy Land and donated large sums of money to help the Jews he found there; his money helped to build the first neighbourhood outside the walls of the Old City. In 1870, the first Jewish agricultural school, Mikve Israel, was established on the outskirts of Jaffa; it still stands there.

Then in 1882, a Russian Jew called Leon Pinsker published a book called *Auto-Emancipation*, suggesting that the Jews should emancipate themselves as other minorities had done. This started the wave of emigration to Palestine from Russia and Romania, spurred on by the terrible pogroms in those countries.

But the greatest impetus to the founding of a homeland for the Jews was the indirect result of the controversial trial of Captain Alfred Dreyfus, in 1894. Dreyfus, a Jew, was accused of treason by the French army, although there was not a shred of evidence that he was the guilty party. The true culprit, a Major Esterhazy, eventually confessed, but even that did not immediately help Dreyfus to be rehabilitated and returned from Devil's Island, where he had been sent in disgrace. It took a fierce campaign against the virulently anti-semitic French authorities to eventually achieve a measure of justice for Dreyfus.

The Dreyfus trial was attended by a young Viennese journalist called Theodor Herzl, who was deeply impressed by the anti-semitic atmosphere in the court and the French press and vowed to do something about it. Herzl can truly be said to be the founder of the Zionist movement. The first Zionist Congress was held under his auspices in Basle in 1897, and the World Zionist Organization was founded with the aim of 'establishing for the Jewish people a publicly and legally assured home in Palestine'.

The early Jewish settlers in Palestine were confronted with a wasteland, sparsely populated by Arab peasants scratching a living from land owned by absentee landlords. Malaria and trachoma were rife in the countryside, tuberculosis in the towns. The first Jewish settlements were established at the end of the 19th century, at Rishon-le-Zion, Zichron Ya'akov and Petah Tikvah, but all needed massive injections of funds from abroad to keep the settlers going. At the same time, Jews began emigrating to the cities of Jerusalem, Jaffa, Haifa and Tiberias and establishing schools and other institutions.

TOP *Early settlers at Gedera, a farming village. Women and men had absolute equality from the first, and shared all the heavy manual labour.*

ABOVE *This classic portrait of the founder of modern Zionism, Theodor Herzl, was taken as he looked out over his hotel balcony at the first Zionist Congress at Basle in 1897. His most famous saying was 'If you wish it, it is not a dream', and his wish for a Jewish state did indeed become a reality, though not in his lifetime.*

THE KIBBUTZ

The kibbutz is undoubtedly the most famous creation of the new Jewish society, created prior to the establishment of the State of Israel, and which continues to flourish. Kibbutz society has probably been studied more closely by ethnologists and sociologists than any other culture. A society in which everything is shared and nothing is individually owned has fulfilled many a utopian ideal, and similar collectives have been established elsewhere – in 19th-century America and in the USSR, for instance – but none has succeeded so spectacularly as the kibbutz in Israel.

The kibbutz is the result of the role played by Jews in the abortive Russian revolution of 1905. Those who fled to Palestine to escape capture founded the first kibbutz, Degania, established in 1909 on the southern shores of the Sea of Galilee. Degania can still be visited today, and the flourishing community has come a long way since a handful of bedraggled settlers set up their tents in a malarial swamp by the lake.

Other, similar communities soon followed. This type of collective living was found to be perfect to combat the hostile terrain, which was marshy where it was fertile, and rocky and arid where it was not. The attacks on neighbouring Jewish farmers by local Arab settlers also encouraged this form of settlement, as did the British policy in the 1920s and 1930s of forbidding settlement on the land. An old Turkish law stated that if a piece of land was

The date harvest at a kibbutz in
the Beth Shean Valley. In the early
1950s, Iraqi date seedlings were
smuggled from Iraq into Israel; since
then, Israeli dates are the largest and
most succulent in the world. The crop
ripens in the autumn at about the time of
the Jewish New Year.

THE DATE HARVEST

• KIBBUTZ LIFE •

Kibbutzim vary in size from a minimum of 60 members to a maximum of 2,000. The biggest kibbutzim, which took the decision to be so large as part of their concept of communal living, are Afikim and Givat Hayim. In addition to actual members, there are many others who live in the kibbutz community, including children and sometimes elderly parents of members who come to live on the kibbutz when they retire. There is always productive work for the elderly, so that they feel part of the community. In addition, there is a wing of the Israel Defence Forces called the *Nahal*, whose task, after initial military training, is to establish new settlements or add to the population of recently formed ones. Most kibbutzim have a Nahal group, either helping to swell the numbers or, on veteran settlements, learning the skills of collective farming before moving on to new land.

BELOW *In kibbutzim near the Lebanese border, children have had to sleep in underground shelters to protect them from bombardment from over the frontier. Children and their facilities need extra protection, since in the past they have been a special target of terrorists.*

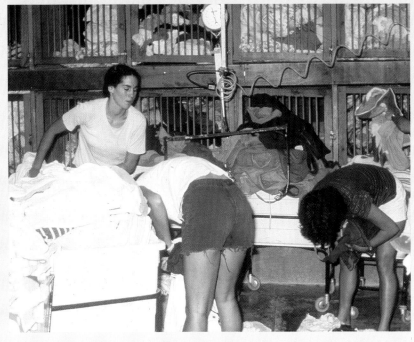

BOTTOM LEFT The kibbutz laundry, where all the members' clothes are washed. Each member has a locker in the clothing store, from which the clean and ironed clothes are collected, and where new clothes may be acquired. In the early days of the kibbutz, all clothing was communally owned! Today, members can ask for new clothing whenever they want it and most kibbutzim have a clothing allowance for members to buy leisure wear in the local town.

TOP LEFT All main meals are eaten together in the kibbutz dining room, although members have stoves and coffee pots in their own homes, where they can prepare and eat snacks and cakes.

ABOVE Kibbutz metalworking factory at Kibbutz Ein Ha'Horesh. Kibbutzim now make a major contribution to the industrial sector, producing high-technology equipment requiring a great degree of skilled labour.

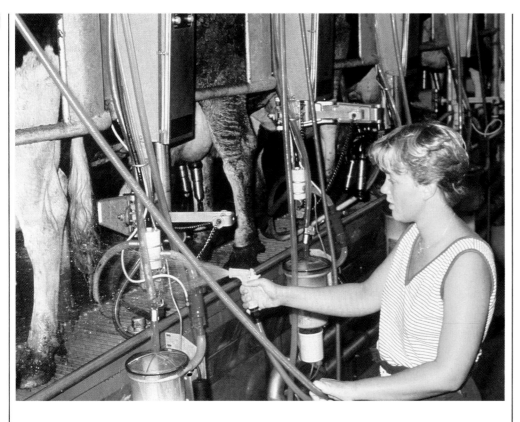

ABOVE A *volunteer working in the milking parlour at Kibbutz Ein Ha-Horesh. Most volunteers study Hebrew for part of the day and work on the kibbutz for the rest of the time. They come from all over the world, and are of all age groups, social classes, races and religions.*

RIGHT *The cotton fields of western Galilee. A happy kibbutznik surveys the crop at Kibbutz Gesher Ha-Ziv, whose members are predominantly from the United States.*

enclosed in the space of one night, the people there had the right to settle on it permanently. (It should not be forgotten that the land in question had already been purchased on behalf of the settlers by the Jewish National Fund.) Thus the 'tower and stockade' movement grew up. Jewish settlers would stealthily move onto the land by night, and by morning they would have erected a sturdy fence and a watchtower.

Kibbutzim have evolved over the years, and there has been more private ownership – of personal clothing, for instance – but in general, the members live in their own quarters but work together in the fields and eat their main meals in a communal dining hall. The administrative committee, headed by the secretary and treasurer, is elected by the members and there is a weekly meeting of members to take major decisions and hear reports from the committee. Children produced by members live together in communal housing from the age of a few months on many kibbutzim, though there is now a tendency for the children to begin living at home with their parents. This places an extra burden on the women.

Many of the kibbutzim, founded by members who had to live in the most abject poverty for decades, are now prosperous com-

munities with swimming pools and saunas, who offer their members trips abroad and other privileges.

Kibbutzim welcome volunteers from all over the world, but particularly from western Europe and the English-speaking world, on short-term work or work-and-study schemes. People of all ages, though mostly youngsters, spend from three to six months on a kibbutz working as volunteers, sometimes only for half a day while they study Hebrew on the type of course known as an *ulpan* for the rest of the day. They are also taken on trips to explore the rest of Israel. These schemes are run by the Jewish Agency for Israel and the World Zionist Organization, and information on the schemes can be obtained from local branches outside Israel. Thousands of young Americans, British, Australians and Canadians have fond, youthful memories of a few months of kibbutz life, and have thus learned to experience this unique collective lifestyle for themselves.

The kibbutz is a product essentially of 'western' Jewry, and although the original founders of the movement came from Russia and Poland, there are now several kibbutzim whose population is predominantly of English-speaking origin (the Israelis refer to Jews from the English-speaking world as 'Anglo-Saxim'!). These include the kibbutzim of Usha and Lavie (both religious kibbutzim), Gesher Haziv in western Galilee and Kibbutz Sasa in Upper Galilee (both predominantly American), Kefar Giladi in Upper Galilee and Kefar Ha-Nasi where the predominantly British members have their own cricket team.

Today kibbutz members comprise only 2.8 per cent of the population of Israel, but produce 40 per cent of agricultural produce. However, kibbutzim are turning increasingly to industry to increase their output and account for 5 per cent of the country's industrial output (including diamond processing). For instance, Kibbutz Afikim has been manufacturing wood and plastic laminates and various types of chipboard and particle board since before 1948 at its Kelet factory, and Kibbutz Metzer produces a type of aluminium-and-plastic piping for hot and cold water supply systems which can be bent like copper but is far cheaper and more efficient.

Kibbutz members, despite their small numbers, have played a disproportionately large role in Israeli politics; most if not all the ministers in the Labour Party and Mapam (now known as the Ma'arakh) have spent part of their lives on a kibbutz. David Ben-Gurion, Israel's first prime minister, spent his latter days in the kibbutz of Sde Boker in the northern Negev, which he helped to found and there are photos of Golda Meir in her early days in Israel feeding the geese at Kibbutz Merhavia.

RIGHT Plan of Kefar Yehoshua, a moshav founded in 1927 and drawn up by Richard Kaufman, the architect responsible for most of the design of moshavim. The completely circular plan of the first moshav, Nahalal, has been slightly modified to allow for more housing along the access roads.

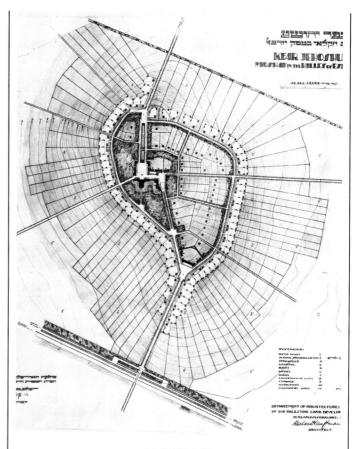

MOSHAV

In 1922, a huge tract of land in the Jezreel Valley was bought from its absentee owners for the then enormous sum of 300,000 Palestine pounds (about $530,000). On a small part of this land, the first cooperative village, or *moshav*, was founded. It was called Nahalal. The houses were built in a circle for better defence and the aerial view of the Nahalal circle is one of the most famous images of Israel. Today, there are 450 moshavim in Israel, each occupied by an average of 60 families.

The moshav has been more successful as a way of life than the kibbutz, because it is not so radical and allows for more family life and privacy. Each member is given a house, essential furniture (unless he or she already has it) and a tract of land. The farming members collectively discuss what to grow and share the cost and use of heavy machinery and processing plants, packing station and so on, for their crops. If any members go to work outside the moshav, a proportion of what they earn is paid to the central moshav committee to cover the village overheads. While the kibbutzim are settled in the main by native-born Israelis, immi-

ABOVE *Mitzpeh Harduf in Galilee, one of the new types of settlement in the West Bank and other areas hitherto inhabited mainly by Arabs. The idea is to establish a Jewish presence in the area for security reasons. The members cultivate land but also work in neighbouring towns; they live in family units.*

grants from Europe and others brought up in a socialist tradition, the moshavim are inhabited by Jews from a very wide variety of backgrounds. Moshavniks range from middle-class emigrants from Germany and Austria to North African shopkeepers and Yemenite craftsmen, all of whom have decided to become farmers in their homeland.

MOSHAV-SHITUFI

There are only 45 moshavim-shitufi'im settlements in Israel, the first of which, Kefer Hittim, was founded in 1936. They combine features of the kibbutz, such as collective farming of the land and pooling of resources, with those of the moshav, such as private family dwellings (owned by the village) and the children being raised at home. However, earnings from the outside are pooled and each family is allocated enough money to live on, based on family size. Like the kibbutz, the moshav-shitufi has a 'culture room', a community centre containing a hall where plays and films are shown and members can gather for a drink and to read newspapers. A total of 7,000 people live on a moshav-shitufi.

MITZPEH

In the 1980s a new form of Jewish settlement was established, the *mitzpeh*, or lookout post. This is a village in the traditional, Euro-

pean sense, without formal collectivization. Most of these settlements have been established in the West Bank (Judaea and Samaria) and in the Golan Heights, though there are a few in Galilee. All are in strategic positions overlooking Arab settlements.

FROM THE 1920s TO INDEPENDENCE The turning-point for Jewish settlement came at the end of World War I, when the Balfour Declaration implicitly stated that Jews were welcome in the soon-to-be British mandated territory of Palestine. Although the British later bitterly regretted their generosity, it gave new impetus to Jewish settlement. Herzl's dream city of Tel-Aviv had been founded in 1909. From a sand dune near Jaffa, it burgeoned into a flourishing city in its own right. As the 1920s and 1930s progressed and latent anti-semitism turned to overt anti-semitism in Europe, Jews from Russia, Poland and the German-speaking countries flocked to the city, trying to make it a replica of the Old World capitals they had left behind. The arts flourished, theatres and concert halls were established and there were even opera and ballet companies.

Jewish immigration ground to a halt in the early 1930s as Arab pressure mounted on the British to stop the return of the Jews. Even after 1945 and the revelation to the world at large of the horrors of World War II and the attendant Holocaust in which 6,000,000 Jews were systematically exterminated (although the Great Powers were probably well aware of the Jewish plight under the Nazis from the beginning), the British tried to stop immigration and sent Jewish immigrant ships back to Germany. During this period an *Aliyah Bet*, or illegal immigration network, was set up, which smuggled many refugees to Israel, saving them from certain death.

INDEPENDENCE AND IMMIGRATION The British finally gave up the struggle of trying to adjudicate between Jew and Arab and threw in the towel. They withdrew on 14 May 1948, hoping the vacuum they left would be filled by invading Arab armies. They were out of luck. The Jews managed to throw off the Arab attacks, though they lost their homes in the Old City of Jerusalem and many other settlements in what is now the West Bank. In 1948, in Tel-Aviv, David Ben-Gurion read out Israel's Declaration of Independence. He became the first prime minister; Chaim Weizmann became the country's first president.

MASS IMMIGRATION IN THE 1940s AND 1950s Israel's independence was the signal for a wave of immigration so large that no country has ever experienced anything similar. Jews forced

ABOVE *The first survivors of the death camps coming ashore in Israel. Sociological studies have since shown that the survivors of the Nazi Holocaust who emigrated to Israel adapted to post-war life better than anywhere else in the world, even in their native countries.*

ABOVE RIGHT *Illegal immigrants successfully landing in Palestine. Most of the ships which brought them were barely seaworthy and often sank when intercepted, with loss of life. The illegal landings mostly took place at night in hazardous conditions in out-of-the way places, and the immigrants were taken to kibbutzim where they could remain undetected by the British.*

out by the Arabs poured in from Egypt, Iraq and Syria and from the Yemen, Algeria, Morocco and Tunisia. Displaced persons from the camps of Europe came to join them. The Jewish population of Israel doubled in four years, from 650,000 at the time of the Declaration of Independence, to 1,400,000 in 1952. In 1950, Israel officially passed the Law of Return, a law unique in the history of legislation, giving every Jew the automatic right to citizenship as soon as he or she sets foot in the country.

The immigrants were housed in tent cities and huts called *ma'abarot*, 'temporary shelters'. Mass immigration continued into the 1950s. These years are known to Israelis as the 'austerity period'. Imports were confined to the barest essentials, everything possible was locally made, there was rationing of commodities such as sugar and flour. Gradually, towards the end of the 1950s, life be-came easier. The dangerous primus stove, the only cooking equip-ment available to Israeli housewives, was gradually replaced by the two- and four-burner gas cooker run on bottled gas, though ovens were a rarity until well into the 1960s. The substitute for an oven, used for baking cakes and sometimes for stews, was the wonder-pot, a large ring mould (tube pan) with a vented lid which sat on top of the burner. Instead of a grill (broiler) there was a deep frying-pan (skillet) whose lid contained an electrical heating ele-ment. Winter heating was by kerosene stove; a few wealthy Jerusalemites had central heating. At least starvation, which had

threatened Jerusalem during the 1948 siege, was averted.

The cost of such immigration has been tremendous in financial terms and could never have been achieved without the enormous aid received from Zionist organizations abroad, especially in the United States, such as the United Jewish Appeal and the Jewish National Fund, whose annual budgets are in the hundreds of millions of dollars. In 1983, for instance, the United Jewish Appeal collected $326.5 million for Israel. The Jewish National Fund, orig-inally established to buy land for Jews to settle on in Palestine and later in Israel, has planted more than 200 million trees in Israel, and has an annual budget of more than $160 million spent on 400 different projects within Israel's borders. In addition to afforest-ation, some of this money goes to improving roads and various types of land reclamation. The land reclamation techniques pion-eered by the Jewish National Fund have been adopted in many developing countries.

JEWISH IMMIGRATION TODAY The 1960s, 1970s and 1980s saw more Jews emigrating from western Europe (they had only trickled in before) as well as increasing numbers from eastern Europe, including the USSR, who had been trapped in their coun-tries of origin by Communist anti-Zionism.

Of the four million or so Jews in Israel today, the majority are native-born. The rest come from every continent and every part

LEFT *Kindergarten in a tent city (ma'abara) for new immigrants, in 1948. The Israel Defence Forces, and particularly the women soldiers, did much to help settle in the newcomers, teaching both children and adults.*

OPERATION MAGIC CARPET

The absorption and integration of Jews from backward countries such as the Yemen and Ethiopia have been a major challenge. Yemenite Jews *walked* the thousand or so miles to Palestine in several waves of immigration from the late 19th century, as soon as they heard of renewed Jewish settlement in the land. All of the 45,200 Jews remaining in the Yemen were brought out in Operation Magic Carpet, the Israeli airlift in 1949.

At the time, the Yemen was still stuck in the Middle Ages. There were no paved roads, cars or telephones. The Yemenites felt cold in the planes, so one group decided to light a fire! Yet today, there are Yemenite Jews in important positions in Israeli life. Children of the original immigrants are diplomats, physicians and lawyers as well as skilled craftsmen and farmers. Yemenite-Jewish culture and art have had a profound influence on Israeli life, and Yemenite-inspired music, dance and handicrafts have played a vital role in the development of a uniquely Israeli culture. About 121,500 Iraqi Jews were rescued at the same time, under Operation Ezra and Nehemia (named for the scribe and the prophet who brought the Jews back from Babylonian exile 2,500 years ago).

TOP *A Yemenite Jew in traditional dress stands proudly in front of the Western Wall in Jerusalem. The Yemenites were very observant, and were the only non-European Jews to wear the sidelocks called* peyot *in Hebrew. They are worn by men to carry out in accordance with the biblical injunction not to cut the hair at the corners of the face.*

LEFT *A miniature exodus of the few Jews who remained in the Yemen took place in March 1963, when Yemenite Jews were smuggled out of the country by ship and taken up the Red Sea to the port of Eilat. Immigration from countries hostile to Israel has always been a risky business, and is still conducted under conditions of upmost secrecy.*

RIGHT *Ethiopian Jewish children at play in Israel. Their parents may still wear the elegant traditional dress of the Falashas, a white-draped robe with a narrow, brightly coloured border, but children everywhere prefer tee-shirts and jeans!*

of the globe, but can be divided into the three major communities of Jews – Ashkenazic, Sephardic and Oriental. The Ashkenazic Jews derive their name from the biblical name for a country called Ashkenaz, which is believed to refer to Germany. These Jews originated from the lands of the Holy Roman Empire, eastern France, Germany, Poland and western Russia. Many later emigrated to points north and west, such as Great Britain and the Commonwealth countries, and even more left for the United States, especially in the 19th century. Once in the majority, they have now been overtaken in numbers by Sephardic and Oriental Jews, who originate from the lands of the Ottoman Empire, that is, the Arab countries, western USSR, Greece, Turkey and Yugoslavia. The Sephardic Jews are those who originally fled from the Spanish Inquisition (*Sepharad* is the biblical name for Spain), and who mingled with the Oriental Jews, who had settled in those countries long before (as in the case of the Iraqi Jews, who claim descent from the Babylonian exiles). In general, Sephardic Jews still speak the language of their forefathers, Judezmo, also known as Ladino, a Spanish-based Jewish language. Many Ashkenazim still speak Yiddish, a Jewish language based on Middle German.

Despite their small numbers in the population, Jews from the English-speaking world, the only ones who have consistently emigrated out of idealism and not through persecution and desperation, have played a major role in Israeli life. Only 57,000 or so Jews have come from the United States and Canada, but they have given Israel a prime minister (Golda Meir), a minister of foreign

affairs (Moshe Arens), a minister of agriculture (Dov Joseph), as well as many other senior government officials. Abba Eban, foreign minister for many years under the Labour Alignment government and its predecessors, was born in South Africa and educated in Britain, and Moshe Rosetti, secretary to the Knesset for 30 years, was another British immigrant. The president of the State of Israel, Chaim Herzog, comes from one of the smallest but most active English-speaking Jewish communities; he hails from Dublin where his father was Chief Rabbi of Ireland.

ABSORPTION AND INTEGRATION It has not been easy for German professors to live side-by-side with Libyan cave-dwellers and Viennese doctors, to start life in Israel in a muddy tent with neighbours as varied as Hong Kong shipping executives, Yemenite tinsmiths, Polish engineers, Tunisian shopkeepers and Romanian psychiatrists. In the 1960s, the tent camps gave way to well-appointed absorption centres, where families can gradually get acclimatized to their new surroundings and learn the language and customs of their new country.

Many of these new immigrants became farmers in kibbutzim or moshavim. The vast majority settled in the towns, especially in the development towns set up in the underpopulated parts of the country in the 1950s and 1960s. This is when the northernmost town of Kiryat Shemona was built, and the desert towns south of Beer-Sheba, such as Dimona, Arad and Kiryat Gat.

More recently the Falasha, black Ethiopian Jews, have exchanged their thatched huts for the glass and concrete of Israeli development towns, particularly Beer-Sheba, and are learning the wonders of modern life, such as how to use the telephone and travel by inter-urban bus. Although a few Falashas had been brought to Israel in the past, most of the remaining 32,000 were airlifted out of famine-stricken Ethiopia in 1985, under Operation Moses. Only 10,000 remain in Ethiopia. The Museum of the Diaspora in Tel-Aviv has mounted a permanent exhibition showing how the Falasha lived, and still live, in Ethiopia, and there are young Falashas at the exhibition ready to explain their culture to visitors.

The welding of these vastly different groups of people into one nation has not always gone smoothly. There are cultural divides between Jews from the east and the west, and particularly between ultra-orthodox Jews and the secular population. Yet, as sociologists from all over the world have discovered, there is an essential but intangible element which can only be described as Jewish consciousness which binds Jewish Israelis, native-born and immigrant, together into a 'nation among the nations'.

ABOVE A group of Jews from Bokhara in central Asia, wearing traditional dress. These weavers of Bokharan carpets arrived in Israel in 1948 from their homeland continuing their craft in their adopted land.

TOP A woman from Cochin, southern India, poses in her garden near Beer-Sheba. This tiny community, which is of unknown origin, wears Indian dress, but has a deep attachment to the Jewish faith. Although most of the community has left Cochin, a remnant still lives there, maintaining the synagogue.

ABOVE A young family from Djerba, an island off the Tunisian coast, whose Jewish community dates back to the days when Tunisia was part of Carthage.

• JEWISH TYPES •

ABOVE Moroccan immigrants from the
Atlas Mountains wearing traditional
dress. Most Moroccan town-dwelling
Jews wear modern dress, but these Jews
are from the interior, known as the
bled. The man also wears a harness, the
tool of his trade, for he is a porter. These
human beasts of burden could carry
phenomenally heavy loads.

JEWISH IMMIGRATION TO ISRAEL AT A GLANCE

EUROPE

Romania	260,188
USSR	199,467
Poland	168,533
Bulgaria	39,887
Hungary	28,175
Czechoslovakia	23,459
France	21,702
United Kingdom	19,798
Germany	15,649
Rest of Europe	37,009
Total	813,867

AMERICAS AND AUSTRALASIA

North America	57,832
Argentina	32,670
Rest of America and Australasia	25,260
Total	115,762

ASIA

Iraq	129,497
Iran	69,755
Turkey	60,134
Yemen	46,411
Indian sub-continent	24,789
Rest of Asia	26,644
Total	357,230

AFRICA

Algeria	184,413
Morocco	140,365
Libya	35,778
Ethiopia	32,000
Egypt and Sudan	30,002
Tunisia	14,703
South Africa	11,918
Rest of Africa	13,566
Total	462,745

EVERY SIXTH ISRAELI

LEFT *Arab village market. Not all Arabs dress in this colourful and picturesque way; most of the town-dwelling Arabs, especially the younger generation, are indistinguishable from their fellow Israelis.*

66

'Behold, I will extend peace to her like a river, and
the Gentiles like a flowing stream.'

ISAIAH 66:12

'And it shall come to pass, that ye shall divide it by
lot for an inheritance unto you, and to the strangers
that sojourn among you, which shall beget children
among you; and they shall be unto you as born in
the country among the children of Israel.'

EZEKIEL 47:22

IT IS RARELY REALIZED that Israel, even within its pre-1967 borders, has a large non-Jewish population. In fact, every sixth Israeli is a non-Jew. This is yet another contribution to the enormous cultural diversity of Israel.

Non-Jews living in Israel proper number 710,000, having increased from only 140,000 when Israel became independent in 1948. Some of this increase has occurred through the annexation of East Jerusalem and its surrounding villages after the 1967 Six Day War. Although not all regard themselves as Arabs, they are mainly Arabic-speaking, and Arabic has the joint status of an official

RIGHT *The marketplace in Bethlehem. These women wear their beautiful local costume on a daily basis. Each town or village has its own particular colour scheme and pattern.*

RIGHT *Street scene in the Old City of Jerusalem. Arab peasants, both men and women, still prefer to carry heavy burdens on their heads.*

68

language, with Hebrew. The non-Jewish citizens of Israel have the same rights as the Jewish citizens and are subject to the same kind of nationality laws as other countries have, meaning that they can acquire nationality by birth or by naturalization. However, the 1,500,000 or so inhabitants of the West Bank and the Gaza Strip remain in a controversial political limbo, cut off from their former countries of Jordan and Egypt by the boundary changes after the Six Day War, but not part of Israel, since annexation would cause such fierce international reaction against Israel. Local elections can, however, be held in the West Bank and the Gaza Strip, and the mayors of the main towns are usually regarded as the political spokesmen for the Arabs in the territories.

There have been Arabs in Israel, both town-dwelling and nomadic Bedouin, since ancient times. It is possible to identify tribes such as the Ammonites and the Idumeans mentioned in the Bible as being Arabs. Over the centuries, some of these tribes, such as the Idumeans, converted to Judaism; others did not adopt monotheism until the coming of Christianity, and some of these Christians converted to Islam. Palestine was under Arab rule for more than five hundred years (from AD 637 to 1071) and these Arabs were replaced by the Seljuk Turks, who were also Moslem, in 1071. After a brief period under Crusader rule, the Moslem Mamelukes occupied the country from 1291 to 1516. They were replaced by the Ottoman Turks whose rule lasted until 1917, so the land has been under Moslem rule for 1,300 years, though always from abroad. Furthermore, the local Arab population was decimated by the battles within its territory (such as those against the Crusaders), and the lack of work opportunities forced many to emigrate. Arabs actually began to return to Palestine in the wake of the new development following the return of the Jews in the late 19th century.

An unfortunate legacy of Ottoman rule over Palestine is that communities are divided up on the basis of their official religion, though this may not reflect the extent of their piety. In the Middle East as a whole, people are classified in this way politically, and even socially, since first names and family names are an immediate giveaway. A George Khoury could not be anything but an Arab Christian, and a Mohammad Akram Al-Mansour could not be anything but a Moslem.

ISRAELI MOSLEMS

The overwhelming majority of Israel's non-Jewish population is Moslem, mostly Sunni Moslems, with a few Shi'ite and Hanafi Moslems. The Sunnis and Hanafis are less strict than the Shi'ites.

Israeli Moslem women are never veiled, and until recently few were seen wearing the all-enveloping *shador*, or even a head-covering. In fact, just after the Six Day War, Moslem religious leaders of the Old City of Jerusalem expressed the fear that Moslem girls might emulate the then current fashion for miniskirts which was sweeping Israel as it was Europe and America. They were right; miniskirts started appearing on Moslem girls almost immediately! There has, however, been a reversion to the 'traditional' values, in the wake of a worldwide fundamentalism which seems to have embraced all religions in the late 1980s. Particularly in Jerusalem and the West Bank, many young girls are to be seen wearing plain headscarves hiding all their hair, and long, drab garments of grey or beige, occasionally ornamented with tucks and pleats.

This drab dress, affected by town-dwelling Arab women, contrasts sharply with the brightly coloured peasant costumes of the village Arab women. They can be seen flocking to the market in the Old City of Jerusalem to buy or sell wares, dressed in the embroidery styles and colour schemes peculiar to their own villages. The long dresses have a square, cross-stitched yoke, which is sometimes also decorated with couched gold thread, and an intricate border around the skirt hem. The side-seams of the dress are oversewn with multi-coloured bands of satin stitch. A similar style is worn by the Arab women in the two clusters of villages known as the Little Triangle and the Big Triangle, in the Plain of Sharon,

RIGHT *Bedouins eke out a precarious living tending flocks of sheep in the Judaean Desert. Their lifestyle has hardly changed in two thousand years, though they have quickly taken to some of the comforts of modern life, particularly the transistor radio!*

FAR RIGHT *A Bedouin encampment in the northern Negev, near a wadi, or dry river bed. The sprinkling of greenery over the brown soil indicates that this is spring, and rains may soon flood the wadi again so that there will be plenty of water for the flocks.*

BELOW *Bedouin graduate at Ben-Gurion University in the Negev. It is quite common for young Bedouins to retain traditional dress, although their Arab contemporaries abandon it when they go on to higher education.*

near the West Bank town of Kalkilya. However, instead of cotton or linen, these Arab women wear velvet dresses. All wear a long white veil, and as much jewellery as they can afford. The village men wear the white head-covering known as the *keffiyeh* and the black band to hold it in place known as the *akal*.

The town-dwelling Arabs generally dress much like other Israelis, especially if they are Christians. Perhaps the Arab population closest to Jewish life is that of Haifa, where Jews and Arabs have lived side by side for centuries.

The Arabs have their own state-funded school system, and they may attend universities such as the Jewish Hebrew University, or the Arab University of Bir Zeit in the West Bank, as well as other universities abroad. All Arab Israelis are bilingual, speaking Hebrew and Arabic, and many also speak English.

The Moslem holy places in Israel include the Haram As-Sharif (including the Mosque of Oman and El-Aksa Mosque in Jerusalem), the Tomb of the Patriarchs in Hebron and the Mosque of Al-Jazzar in Acre.

THE BEDOUIN These romantic desert-dwellers roam throughout Israel, in Galilee and the West Bank, but mostly in the northern Negev Desert where at least half the population lives. Their low black tents and grazing sheep, goats and camels are a familiar roadside sight in remote areas. There are 67,000 Bedouins in Israel, all divided into tribes. Some sided with Israel during its struggle for independence, fearing repression by the invading forces. Many Israeli Bedouin have decided to settle down in houses, where their children can be educated for the wider opportunities afforded in the towns. The nomads retain their traditional dress of

ARAB CHILDREN

long dark robes. Although the women generally do not bother with the veil, in the presence of a strange man they may partly cover their faces with a thick cloth covered with coins. They wear a small, dark cap under their black veils, decorated with silver or gold coins, and their heavy, silver jewellery is much prized.

THE CIRCASSIANS These Moslems are of European descent, and emigrated from western Russia in 1880. They were brought to Palestine by the Turks, and have settled mostly in two villages in central Galilee, Rihaniye and Kefar Kana. They number about 4,000 people. A few have moved to Jerusalem. Like the Bedouin, the Circassians serve in the Israeli army. They are mostly very European-looking, with golden hair and blue eyes, and they wear European dress.

ISRAELI CHRISTIANS

The majority of Israeli Christians are Greek Catholic. This is a branch of the Greek Orthodox church which split away from the patriarchate and recognizes Rome as the supreme spiritual authority, although the services and ritual are close to orthodoxy. There are almost as many Greek Orthodox Israelis. The next largest community is that of the Maronites. This Christian sect is confined largely to Lebanon, and is part of the Roman Catholic church. It is named after Maro, a monk who lived in Lebanon in the 8th century. Greek Catholics and Maronites pray in Arabic.

The remainder of Israel's Christians are Armenian, Armenian Uniate (Catholic) or Protestant. There are, of course, priests, monks and nuns of almost every Christian denomination living in Israel, but few are citizens. The Christian Arabs live mainly in villages in Galilee, and in Haifa and Jerusalem. Despite much missionary activity by the Protestants from the West, Arab Protestants remain the smallest Arab Christian community. Other Christian sects represented in Israel almost entirely by priests, monks and nuns are Egyptian Copts, Ethiopian Copts, and members of both the Russian Orthodox churches, the church in exile and the church headquartered in Moscow. All are there to look after and run the Christian holy places.

Many of the Christian holy places in Israel are dotted along the Via Dolorosa in Jerusalem, the route Christ took carrying his cross. There is, for instance, the Convent of Ecce Homo, at the First Station, where Pontius Pilate said those famous words, 'Ecce Homo' (Behold, the man), and the Convent of Saint Veronica at the Sixth Station, where Saint Veronica wiped Christ's face with a veil on which the imprint of his face was left.

OPPOSITE *Arab children playing in a street in the Old City of Jerusalem. The girls wear trousers under their skirts to hide their legs, a custom introduced by the Turks. Jewish children from Turkey and the Arab countries are dressed in a similar way.*

RIGHT *Palm Sunday procession in Jerusalem as it passes by the Church of St Mary, where the Virgin Mary is supposed to be buried. In the background above is French Hill.*

BELOW *In the courtyard of the Ethiopian Coptic church in Jerusalem, an old monk sits surrounded by relics of a former Ethiopian church on the site. He is a member of one of the oldest Christian sects.*

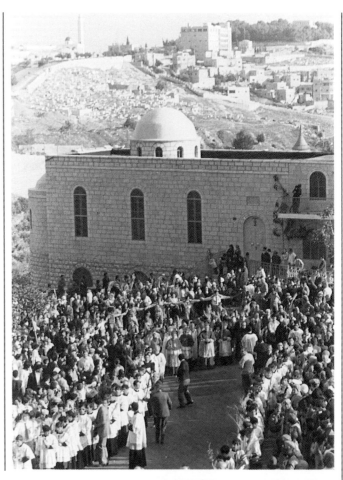

CHRISTIAN HOLY PLACES

Among Christian holy places in Jerusalem are the Church of the Holy Sepulchre which non-Protestants believe to be the site of Golgotha (Protestants believe it to be the Garden Tomb, just outside the present city walls), the Church of the Dormition on Mount Zion (where the Virgin Mary fell into an eternal sleep), on the top of which is the Room of the Last Supper, the Church of St Anne, where Mary's parents are reputed to have lived (a gem of unsullied Crusader architecture) and the Tomb of the Virgin Mary (also outside the city walls, in the Valley of Hinnom just east of Gethsemane). Outside of Jerusalem, there are the Church of the Nativity in Bethlehem, and in Galilee the Church of the Annunciation in Nazareth, as well as three other important sites, the Mount of the Beatitudes, Tabgha, where the multiplication of the loaves and fishes is alleged to have taken place, and Capernaum (Kefar Nahum), where Jesus preached in the synagogue. All these shrines are presided over by one or more Christian denominations, usually Catholic, Armenian and Greek Orthodox. Only one site is administered solely by the Russian Orthodox church, the tomb of St Tabitha, on the outskirts of Jaffa.

RIGHT *The Arch of Ecce Homo in Jerusalem, the First Station of the Cross on the Via Dolorosa. Here Pontius Pilate is said to have shown Jesus to the people and declared 'Behold, I bring him forth to you' (John 19:4).*

BELOW *The Church of the Holy Sepulchre in Jerusalem, which most Christian sects believe to be Golgotha, the site of the Crucifixion and burial. Although now within the city walls, it was outside them in Christ's time.*

RIGHT In the Grotto of the Nativity, Bethlehem. The Church of the Nativity is shared between the Greek Orthodox, Roman Catholic and Armenian churches, each of which tends a different part of the building. The church stands in the centre of the town in Manger Square.

LEFT The Church of the Annunciation in Nazareth. Although Nazareth is full of churches and Christian shrines, most of today's Nazarenes are Moslems.

ABOVE The ruined synagogue at Capernaum (Kefar Nahum). These remains date from the 6th century, but Christ preached in an earlier synagogue on the same site.

RIGHT *A Druze elder. The Druze live in villages on Mount Carmel and in the Golan Heights. Their religion is kept secret from outsiders and even within their ranks not all are initiated into the most sacred rites. The religion is an offshoot of Islam, but women are granted a more equal status.*

OPPOSITE *The golden dome of the Baha'i Shrine in Haifa is illuminated at night, and makes a magnificent sight. The Baha'is are a religious group whose leader, the Baha'ullah, came from Persia and is buried here. Unfortunately, there are few Baha'is left in Iran because of persecuting; most live in the United States. Almost every Baha'i makes a pilgrimage at least once to the Baha'ullah's grave.*

THE DRUZE

The Druze religion is shrouded in secrecy and mystery and is only known to initiates (who include women). In fact, it is a breakaway religion from Islam which is believed to have something in common with the Ismaili version of the faith. The Israeli Druze have shown a surprising empathy with their Jewish neighbours and serve with distinction in the Israeli army. They serve mainly as Border Guards, wearing the distinctive green berets of the frontier regiments.

The Druze live almost exclusively in a collection of villages on the leeward side of Mount Carmel and in the Carmel range of mountains, as well as on the Golan Heights. Their distinctive white dress and the rounded white turbans of the men are often to be seen in the streets of Haifa, though most young Druze dress identically to their Jewish compatriots.

THE BAHA'I

Although the Baha'is number only a few hundred in Israel, the fact that their holy shrine is located in Haifa makes it important to mention them. The Baha'ullah, prophet and founder of the Baha'i faith, was born in Persia (now Iran) in the early 19th century. The shrine consists of a golden-domed temple and a museum and archive in classical Greek style, set in beautifully maintained gardens marked out with hedges and tall cypress trees. The Baha'i Shrine is as much a sight typical of Haifa as the Mosque of Oman's golden dome is typical of Jerusalem.

THE KARAITES

Although Judaism claims to have no sects, there are two religions which have close affinities to Judaism, one of which – Karaism – deserves the name of sect. Marriage between Karaites and Jews is recognized by the Israeli rabbinate, and such marriages may take place in a synagogue. Since no non-Jew may marry in a synagogue, the Karaites are tacitly admitted to be Jews.

The Karaites do not accept the teachings of the Talmud, and reject rabbinic tradition. They take the Bible teachings literally, so that, for instance, they do not allow themselves any light or heat on the Sabbath. There are 15,000 Karaites in Israel; they live mainly in Ramla, Ashdod and Beer-Sheba, and hail mainly from the Crimean Peninsula and Egypt, where the Karaite faith gained the most adherents. The Knesset member and well-known spokesperson for women's and citizens' rights, Shulamit Aloni, is of Karaite extraction.

THE SAMARITANS

Of all the minority communities in Israel, the Samaritans are the most enigmatic and fascinating. They claim to be the descendants of the Lost Tribes of the sons of Joseph, Manasseh and Ephraim, but they are probably descended from the Jews left behind in Judah when the Jews were taken into exile by the Babylonians. They have their own version of the Five Books of Moses and the Book of Joshua, written in an archaic form of Hebrew. Over the centuries, they have repeatedly denied any connection with Jews or Judaism, especially when the Jews were being persecuted. Yet their faith and practices resemble Judaism more closely than any other religion.

There are two Samaritan communities, one in Israel proper, at Holon on the outskirts of Tel-Aviv, and the other centred near the Samaritan holy place, Mount Gerizim, at Nablus (Shechem) on the West Bank. Both communities number only 250 souls. Their main festival is the Festival of the Sacrifice, celebrated at the time of the Jewish Passover (around Easter). Sheep are sacrificed on Mount Gerizim, then cooked in a huge pit and eaten.

The Samaritan attitude to the State of Israel is somewhat ambivalent, though as the Secretary of the Community once stated 'We could never have accepted the State had it been called anything but Israel – Judah for instance'. This reflects a 2,500-year-old grudge! The Samaritans look and dress like other Israelis, but even if religious, do not cover their heads like Jews, since this is a recently adopted Jewish tradition.

All the minority communities in Israel have freedom of worship and their holy places are protected under Israeli law. Some are represented in the Knesset by their own leaders, others prefer to vote for the mainly Jewish political parties. In addition to their cultural influence on the Israeli community, their contribution as farmers, herdsmen and skilled workers has proved to be very important.

ISRAEL'S MINORITY COMMUNITIES

Moslems (including 67,000 Bedouin) 546,700 (76.5 per cent)
Christians 95,850 (13.4 per cent)
Druze 53,000 (7.4 per cent)
Karaites 15,000 (2.1 per cent)
Circassians 4,000 (0.5 per cent)
Samaritans 500 (250 on West Bank) (0.1 per cent)

Total: 715,050

A SENSE OF HISTORY

LEFT *Studying archaeology at the Hebrew University in Jerusalem. Israelis are avid seekers after their own past, and it is only since Israel became a sovereign state that they have been able to excavate some of the most interesting sites, such as Jerusalem.*

78

'Remove not the ancient landmark, which thy
fathers have set.'

PROVERBS 22:28

FEW NATIONS can be so conscious of their
own past while ever striving towards the future as
the Israelis. They are one of the oldest nations in
the world, yet one of the newest, whose rich
traditions have only survived against incredible
odds due to constant evolution and change.

In Israel, the past is all around and underfoot. There are certain
parts of the country, around Caesarea, Afula and Acre, for instance, where local people make it a habit of looking for ancient
coins after the winter rains, and archaeological finds are almost
commonplace. Amazing discoveries have been made by amateurs.
In 1975, a New York stockbroker on vacation used a metal detec-
tor and a penknife to unearth a magnificent bronze bust of the
Emperor Hadrian. A Belgian millionaire, Theo Siebenberg, built
himself a house in Jerusalem with foundations designed so that he
could excavate under the building. He has found hundreds of
artefacts dating from the 1st century AD all the way back to a
burial chamber from the First Temple Period, in 900 BC. Siebenberg
is building a museum in which to display his finds. Among the
prominent Israelis who have owned important private archaeology collections were the former government minister and
deputy prime minister, Yigal Allon, and General Moshe Dayan.

All the nations who conquered, occupied and lived in the Holy
Land have left their mark. There are 3,500 registered archaeological sites in Israel. Although before the establishment of the state
many of the best finds were taken out of the country (for instance, by the London-based Palestine Exploration Society) since
the establishment of the state all important finds have remained in
the country. Sites such as Hatzor, Avdat and Arad in the Negev,
Caesarea on the Mediterranean, Masada in the Judaean desert and
Tel Dan in northern Galilee at one of the sources of the Jordan,
have all been excavated by Israeli archaeologists, working through
the Israel Department of Antiquities. Priority is given to sites
which are in danger of being destroyed by new buildings.

Sites from all periods have been excavated, starting as early as a
neolithic site in Jericho (about 7500 BC), and chalcolithic sites in the
Golan Heights and Mount Carmel (about 6000 BC); one unique find
was the presence of skeletons of both Neanderthal man and

ABOVE One of the ancient sites of
Jericho. This city is probably the oldest
constantly inhabited site on earth.
Although various walled cities have
been unearthed there, the city walls
destroyed by Joshua and his army have
yet to be found.

RIGHT Detail of the mosaic pavement of
the 6th-century church at Kissufim. This
early Byzantine church is one of the
oldest of all places of worship. The
mosaic depicts Alexander the Great, who
is alleged to have visited the Holy Land,
though no proof of his visit exists.

'ASTARTE' FIGURES – 8TH–6TH CENTURIES BC

80

LEFT A *beautiful mosaic depicting two hinds and the Tree of Life at the Palace of King Hisham at Jericho. The artist was probably a Byzantine working for the new Arab conquerors.*

RIGHT *The most controversial archaeology project – but by far the most important for Jewish historians – is the 15-year plan to excavate the area south of Temple Mount. Despite objections from all religious groups and the Arab states, the project has gone ahead and yielded finds of enormous importance. The foreground shows a house from the Byzantine period.*

LEFT *The Western Wall, Jerusalem, originally the Western Wall of the Second Temple (destroyed AD 70). In 1967, the Wall, formerly known as the Wailing Wall, stood in a narrow alley surrounded by houses. When the houses were removed, finds dating back to the time of the first Temple (10th to 6th century BC) were uncovered.*

Homo sapiens man in the same cave on Mount Carmel, the only time both types of early man have ever been found together.

Many archaeological sites are open to the public. The best known is, of course, Masada, in the Judaean desert, which has been discussed elsewhere in this book. Sites on the West Bank, previously inaccessible before the Six Day War, include another of Herod's fortresses, Herodion, and the wealth of archaeological treasures of Jericho, which is considered to be the oldest continuously inhabited site in the world. Of particular interest to visitors to Jericho, under the shadow of the Mount of Temptation, where the Devil is supposed to have tempted Christ, are the ruins of the magnificent palace of Hisham Abd-el-Malik, one of the first Arab rulers of the area. Kathleen Kenyon, the distinguished British archaeologist, first began excavations in the oldest part of Jericho at Tel Es-Sultan. The word *Tel* in a place name indicates an ancient mound covering archaeological remains, except in the case of Tel-Aviv, a name invented by Theodor Herzl to imply a mixture of the old and new, since *Aviv* means 'spring'. The distinct types of New Stone Age cultures dating from the 8th century BC have been found in Jericho, as well as the earliest permanent houses in the Holy Land. They were built of brick and had rounded roofs, much as some Arab houses are built today.

It is worth noting that although Jericho has had many walls surrounding it at various times in its history, many of which were destroyed, archaeologists have been unable to identify the one which fell down during Joshua's battle to capture the city, when the trumpets blared and the Israelites gave out a great shout (Joshua 2:1).

Fascinating examples of life in Jerusalem from the First Temple Period to Roman times can be seen in the Old City of Jerusalem and its environs. Excavations on the southern side of Temple Mount have revealed continuous settlement dating back to the time of King Solomon (967–928 BC) and forward to the times of the Umayyad (Arab) Caliphs of the 8th century AD, who built palaces there. Reconstruction work in the Jewish Quarter has revealed excavations dating back to the First Temple Period (10th to 6th century BC). There are also remains of houses destroyed by fire when the Romans sacked and burned Jerusalem in AD 70. Sections of the Cardo, the magnificent colonnaded Roman thoroughfare that ran through the centre of the Old City, have been discovered and reconstructed. The Nea (New St Mary's) church, built by the Emperor Justinian in the 6th century, has also been uncovered. The Roman city of Jerusalem, as it looked in Herod's day, has been reconstructed in miniature and can be visited in the grounds of the Holyland Hotel in the west Jerusalem suburb of Bayit Ve-Gan.

LEFT *Artefacts taken from the Cave of the Letters, where letters from the Jewish general and rebel, Simon Bar-Kochba, were found, dating from AD 132-135. The jugs and mirrors are of bronze. The wooden knife handle and mirror-back are reconstructions.*

BELOW *Part of the copper hoard found in the Judaean Desert where Simon Bar-Kochba and his followers hid from the Romans during the Jewish Revolt of AD 132-135. The cave in which these objects were found is known as the treasure cave. It is not known what these objects were used for.*

LEFT *A scale model of Jerusalem in the time of King Herod, laid out in the grounds of the Holyland Hotel in the Jerusalem suburb of Bayit Ve-Gan. Herod the Great erected a huge number of buildings all over his realm, including in his capital. His works in Jerusalem included the Fortress of Antonia and considerable alterations to the Temple, but this did not endear him to his subjects, who saw him as a paranoid despot and a lackey of the Romans.*

The city was a completely different shape from today, and benefited from Herod's grandiose buildings, the Fortress of Antionia and Herod's palace, which attempted to outshine the Temple.

Since the Six Day War many sites of Jewish and Christian interest have been found on the Golan Heights, dating from the Second Temple period and continuing right into Byzantine times (4th century AD). These have been partially restored, so one can now see these synagogues, Talmudic academies and early churches and monasteries and imagine how they looked centuries ago.

MUSEUMS

There are 22 museums in Israel which are either devoted in part or as a whole to archaeology; the Israel Museum is the largest. Smaller museums with interesting exhibits include the Rockefeller Museum, just outside the the Old City of Jerusalem, and Ein Harod Museum on Kibbutz Ein Harod in Lower Galilee – both

quite fascinating. The Hecht Museum inside the Haifa University campus and the Haifa Museum of Prehistory (established in 1976) have spectacular collections.

Items on display include mosaics, artefacts, all sorts of vessels and particularly glass. Glass is a speciality of the Eretz-Israel Museum, founded in 1953, at Ramat Aviv, just north of Tel-Aviv, on the opposite bank of the Yarkon River. Israel probably has the most magnificent collections of ancient glass in the world, since it was the Phoenicians, who inhabited what is today northern Israel and Lebanon, who discovered the art of glassmaking. Vessels of amazing intricacy include coloured glass and 'gold-glass', two sheets of glass enclosing a stencil-type pattern cut in gold leaf, a style which was popular in Roman times. The Eretz-Israel Museum also has Israel's most important collection of ancient coins.

There are also many fine examples of mosaic flooring from late Roman synagogues and churches, including the ancient church at Tabgha on the Sea of Galilee depicting loaves and fishes to com-

84

memorate Jesus' miracle, and the magnificent depiction of the zodiac and the sacrifice of Isaac in the 6th century AD synagogue at Bet Alpha in the same area. Perhaps the most significant Christian find is the stone inscription found in Caesarea, now in the Israel Museum, which contains the only reference to Pontius Pilate outside the Bible.

The most important discovery of Jewish interest is unquestionably the Dead Sea Scrolls. These were found by an Arab shepherd in a cave at Qumran near the Dead Sea in 1947, just before Israel's War of Independence. Their existence was long kept secret, and they were not displayed to the public until a special building, the Shrine of the Book, was erected to house them near the Israel Museum.

The Shrine of the Book and the Israel Museum complex were both opened in 1965.

The scrolls, the oldest manuscripts in the Hebrew language, were written in about 100 BC. There are so many of them that even 40 years later, they are still being studied and deciphered. Since they were found near Qumran, where the Essenes, a Jewish, ascetic sect, had their headquarters, it is assumed that they were buried by the Essenes. In addition to passages from the Bible, which differ in only minor detail from the texts we know today, there are passages from the Apocrypha and Pseudepigrapha (post-

ABOVE *The Shrine of the Book (Heihal Ha-Sefer) at the Israel Museum. The precious scrolls themselves are in an underground chamber beneath this cupola, to protect them from attack.*

● THE MUSEUM OF THE DIASPORA ●

The more recent Jewish past is commemorated in two important museums. Bet Ha-Tefutzot (the Museum of the Diaspora), which attempts to record the whole of Jewish history, both in Israel and the Diaspora, is located just north of Tel-Aviv, on the campus of Tel-Aviv University. This unique project, established in 1978 by Dr Nahum Goldmann of the World Jewish Congress, does not contain a single genuine artefact. It consists entirely of replicas, mockups, models and audiovisual displays, depicting Jewish life through the ages in every country which has had even the tiniest Jewish community. The museum has an archive which is constantly in the process of collecting material on Jewish communities, especially as they are tending to disappear as their members emigrate elsewhere, and on Jewish surnames and their origins. Visitors to the museum can use computer searches to find out information about a particular community or surname.

ABOVE *The Museum of the Diaspora, in Ramat-Aviv near Tel-Aviv University, is devoted exclusively to the history of Jewish culture and civilization. All of the exhibits are replicas or modern representations. Much use is made of audiovisual displays and computerized information. The original aim was to give Israelis a sense of their own past.*

LEFT Jewish life in the ghettos of Poland in the 17th century. The Jewish community of Poland/Lithuania (then one country) was a highly organized one.

BELOW LEFT A visitor inspects a model of the synagogue in Florence, Italy. It still stands, a spectacular reminder of the power of this affluent Jewish community, who built it in the 1880s.

BELOW Replica of the Arch of Titus in Rome, Italy. The triumphal arch shows the Romans carrying away the golden candelabra and other sacred vessels from the Temple in Jerusalem, after it was conquered and destroyed in AD 70.

biblical works written in Aramaic) and texts hitherto unknown, such as the War of the Sons of Light and the Sons of Darkness.

Some of the scrolls are a record of the lives of the Essenes, a Jewish sect that lived near the Dead Sea and fought against the Romans in AD 70, when they were destroyed. There are many other scrolls, all written in Hebrew and Aramaic (the language which Jesus spoke and which was the vernacular in his time; it is similar to Hebrew and uses the same characters).

The Shrine of the Book is an interesting and symbolic piece of architecture. The distinctive exterior is made of glistening white tiles, and is shaped to resemble the lid of one of the stone jars in which the scrolls were found. A selection of the scrolls themselves, fragments from the book of Isaiah, the oldest manuscripts in the Hebrew language, are displayed in the centre of the round building. The whole building is partly sunken into the earth to protect it from attack during war. The scrolls are on an upper floor, displayed in dim light under a cave-like roof. On the lower floor are relics from the Jewish heroes of Masada, and an equally astonishing find, the Bar-Kochba letters, the actual writings of the post-biblical hero, Simon Bar-Kochba, who fought the Romans in the second century AD.

The buildings of the Israel Museum complex are also partly subterranean and have vast underground shelters and storage areas, which would protect the exhibits even from a nuclear attack. The Israel Museum now houses the Bezalel Museum of Art, transferred from the building next door to the Bezalel School of Art when the Museum was opened. The Bezalel Museum has an important collection of Jewish ritual art, including reconstructions of typical synagogues, of which the most interesting are the interiors of a painted wooden Polish synagogue, and the magnificent baroque synagogue from Vittorio Veneto in northern Italy. The Israel Museum also incorporates an archaeological museum, which displays, among other things, Canaanite ossuaries and beautiful golden relics from Persepolis in present-day Iran, dating from the days of the Persian Empire. The Billy Rose Sculpture Garden has large works by leading modern sculptors displayed in the open air, in the spectacular setting of the Judaean Hills.

The Yad Vashem Memorial and Museum in Jerusalem has a sadder purpose. It exists to commemorate the six million Jews who died and even more who suffered at the hands of the Nazis who tried, and almost succeeded, to exterminate European Jewry. Yad Vashem is also the oldest of several Israeli research institutes into the Holocaust period (1933–1945). It runs a project called *Pinkas Ha-Kehillot*, an attempt to carefully reconstruct exactly how the destruction of each Jewish town, village and settlement in

LEFT *Children climbing enthusiastically over a Henry Moore sculpture in the Billy Rose Sculpture Garden of the Israel Museum. The garden contains sculptures by leading European and Israeli sculptors in a spectacular open-air setting with the Judaean Hills in the background.*

OPPOSITE *The ruins of Herod's Palace at Sebastia, capital of Samaria. This town had never had a significant Jewish population, and Herod's choice of it as a site for one of his chain of luxurious palaces built c. 25 BC particularly angered his subjects.*

LEFT *The amphitheatre at Sebastia, another of Herod's constructions. He enjoyed watching fights between wild beasts, another of his barbarous Romanizing activities which made his subjects hate him.*

Nazi-occupied Europe occurred. In this way, a complete picture will eventually emerge of what happened to those millions of victims of insane brutality.

Yad Vashem also has an award scheme to honour the Righteous Gentiles, non-Jews who helped Jews to escape and survive. Recipients of this award are invited to Israel and given a medal and certificate at a ceremony to honour their bravery.

Survivors of that terrible period are everywhere in Israel. You may sit at a sidewalk café in Tel-Aviv and notice that the waitress handing you your glass of tea has a concentration camp number tattooed on her arm; or a grinning shoemender, whose English and Hebrew are thickly accented with Russian, will tell you how he spent two years in eastern Europe fleeing Nazis and Poles alike.

Yet sociologists who have studied survivors of the concentration camps have discovered that they have recovered psychologically far better in Israel than elsewhere, even compared to how non-Jewish survivors have fared upon returning to their own countries. Perhaps it is because in Israel, everyone is a survivor, whether of wars in the distant or the immediate past.

Israel's recent past is commemorated all over the country in many ways, from monuments to the fallen in battle to the fantastically popular 'Treasure Hunt' (*Mehapsim Et Ha-Matmon*) quiz on Israeli radio, which has been running for more than 30 years. The quiz links the studio audience with a 'hunter' and various broadcasters stationed along the route and at the place where the 'treasure' is hidden. The clues are all connected to historical events, usually from the pre-state period of Jewish settlement, and the arbitrator is always a famous Zionist historian.

Israel's rich past, both heroic and tragic, has inspired many recent works of art and architecture, and even has practical applications. Professor Michael Avi-Yonah, who excavated the Nabatean site of Avdat, was interested to see how these desert-dwellers, who lived there in Roman times (and also built the 'rose-red' city of Petra in Transjordan) conserved water in large cisterns. He established an experimental agricultural plot and grew crops in this barren area (the Wilderness of Zin) using the same methods employed by the Nabatean farmers, proving that these age-old methods could be adapted for modern use.

RIGHT *Inside the Ohel Yizkor (the Tent of Remembrance) at the Yad Vashem Memorial to the victims of the Holocaust in Jerusalem. The names of all the concentration and extermination camps are engraved in stone in Latin and Hebrew letters on the floor. The only light source comes from an Eternal Lamp, similar to the one that burns in synagogues.*

MAJOR EVENTS AND RULERS OF THE LAND OF ISRAEL

RULERS	PERIOD
The Patriarchs (Abraham, Isaac, Jacob)	1700–1500 BC
Exodus from Egypt	1300
Reconquest of Canaan by Joshua; the time of the Judges	1200–1000
Kingdom of Saul	1025–1006
Kingdom of David	1006–967
Kingdom of Solomon	967–928
The two kingdoms: Israel and Judah	928–587
The Babylonian Exile	587–539
Return from Babylonia and rebuilding of the Temple under Ezra and Nehemia; Yehud, a province of the Persian Empire	538–332
Conquest by Alexander the Great	332–323
Rule by the Ptolemies	301–198
Rule by the Seleucids	197–164
Hasmonean Dynasty (the Maccabees)	164–37
Roman domination under the House of Herod	37–4
Wars of the Jews and destruction of Jerusalem	AD 68–70
Direct Roman rule	70–313
Byzantine rule (Eastern Roman Empire)	313–636
Arab (Umayyad) rule	637–1091
Seljuk Turkish rule	1091–1098
Crusader domination (the Kingdom of Jerusalem)	1099–1291
Mamelukes of Egypt	1291–1516
Ottoman Turks	1517–1917
British Mandate	1918–1948
State of Israel	1948 to present

HOW ISRAEL
IS RUN

LEFT The Valley of Gehenna in Jerusalem,
looking from the Old City towards the new
city. A sculpture dedicated to the memory of
Israeli soldiers who fell in the Six Day War
dominates the valley.

*'Without counsel purposes are disappointed; but in
the multitude of counsellors they are established.'*

PROVERBS 15:22

NATURALLY, EVERY COUNTRY has a
government structure, a judiciary, police force
(though nowhere else are both the cops and the
robbers mostly Jewish), and so on. However, there
are many aspects of the Israeli political structure
and political life which are unique in the region and even in the
world.

Jews have always been political animals. 'Three Jews, four
opinions', goes the old saying. Nowhere is this more true than in
Israel, which has a constantly changing, merging and splitting ka-
leidoscope of political parties, ranging from the extreme right to
the extreme left, with everything in between.

This is largely because Israel has a system of direct proportional
representation. This means that voting is not for a candidate but
for a party list. Each party is represented at the ballot box by a slip
of paper bearing one or two letters of the Hebrew or Arabic
alphabet. For a party to seat a candidate in the 120-member parliament, known as the Knesset, it must gain a high enough quota of
the votes cast. Parties polling less than 1 per cent of the vote lose
their deposits.

Israel's parliament is run very much on the lines of the British
House of Commons; Israel has a unicameral system, with no upper
house. State functions, such as the attorney general and the gover-
nor of the Bank of Israel, are also modelled on the British system.

Elections are held at least once every four years, but if there is a
vote of no confidence or similar crisis, the cabinet may resign.
Thanks to this unwieldy political system, no political party has yet
won an overall majority in the Israeli parliament, so all of Israel's
governments since 1948 have been coalitions. Partly for this reason,
to accommodate members from all the ruling parties, the cabinet
grew in size from 12 members in 1949 to 24 in 1969, though the
number of ministries only increased from 17 to 20.

After the Six Day War, a so-called National Unity Government
was established, incorporating the two main rival political parties.
The first is the Alignment or Ma'arakh, a group of three socialist
parties, consisting of the Israeli Labour Party (Mapai), a centre-left
party called Ahdut-Ha-Avoda and the left-wing labour Mapam
Party. The other partner in the coalition is the Likud (Alliance),

ABOVE *Entrance to the Knesset building
in Jerusalem. The present building was
constructed in 1965, when the old
Knesset building in the centre of the
western (Jewish) half of the city was
considered too old and shabby. This
rather grandiose structure lacks the
friendly intimacy of the former building,
which is now the Ministry of Tourism.*

RIGHT *Arab (Moslem and Christian)
and Druze members of the Knesset.
Simultaneous translation is provided for
them in Arabic, and they may address
the Knesset in Arabic if they wish.
Arabic is Israel's only other official
language besides Hebrew.*

[Hebrew text of Israel's Declaration of Independence, handwritten]

LEFT *Israel's Declaration of Independence, written and signed (see below) in 1948. This was actually the first time the decision was made as to what the new Jewish State would be called!*

which consists of the right-wing Herut Party and the centre-right Liberal Party.

Attempts at introducing a limited constituency system, especially so that remoter parts of the country would feel they had individual representation in the Knesset, have failed, due to inevitable opposition from the smaller parties. The net result of Israel's extreme proportional representation has been that despite the almost excessive democracy of the voting system, minority parties have such an important role in the balance of power that much legislation has been passed of which the majority of Israelis disapprove. This applies particularly to legislation forcing the non-religious to conform to the standards of orthodox Judaism, such as closing places of entertainment and forbidding television and airline flights on the Sabbath.

The system has also produced a few one-man political parties in its time. One candidate, standing alone, once gained twice the quota of votes and was allocated an extra seat! The smaller parties have over the years represented such diverse elements as the Trotskyite left (Moked), the Yemenites, the Black Panthers of Israel (young Jewish immigrants from the Arab world) and the extreme right (Kach, the Jewish Defence League led by the controversial Meir Kahane). Many countries have a party representing the interests of the religious; Israel has four or more! Officially, the four are the two halves of the Mizrachi movements (Mizrachi and Ha-Poel Ha-Mizrachi) and the two halves of the Agudat Israel movement (Agudat Israel and Poalei Agudat Israel). The halves represent the 'capitalist' and 'socialist' elements, respectively, in their parties; in Mizrachi, the two halves have actually united to form the National Religious Party. Aguda considers itself more orthodox and traditionalist than Mizrachi. For instance, it was the most vociferous in trying to deny women the vote, both in the pre-state and post-state period, and it has done everything in its power to prevent state recognition of Reform and Liberal Judaism. The Agudat Israel leader, Menahem Porush, once tore up a Reform prayerbook and threw it on the floor of the Knesset.

Israel's minorities have their own parties, several of which are linked to the Labour Alignment. However, many choose to vote for existing parties, especially the Communist party, or more correctly for one of the two Communist parties, the Stalinist one (Maki), as the best way of showing dissent from Israeli rule.

Israelis may vote from the age of 18 but may only sit as Knesset members from the age of 21. Debates are conducted in Hebrew, but members from the minority communities may address the Knesset in Arabic, and simultaneous translation is provided.

When a party has enough seats in the Knesset to form and lead

a government, it chooses a prime minister from among its elected members. The president of the State of Israel is elected by the Knesset itself, generally by consensus, and may serve for up to two five-year terms. His role is mainly ceremonial as a head of state, much like a constitutional monarch.

THE ISRAELI LEGAL SYSTEM

Israel's Declaration of Independence grants basic equality to all citizens. In addition, certain Basic or Founding Laws were passed in the early 1950s, to lay down rules for the appointment of the judiciary, the voting system and so on. However, most Israeli law is based on the legislative systems of the two previous rulers of the land, the Ottoman Turks and the British.

As has already been said, the Ottoman Turks divided their subjects into religious communities. They allowed each community a measure of autonomy, as a sort of escape valve for unrest. This system has been perpetuated in Israel as far as personal status is concerned. This means that in matters of marriage and divorce, for instance, each Israeli is subject to the dictates of religious law, the *Bet Din* for the Jews, the *Shariya* for the Moslems and the various ecclesiastical courts for the Christians. There is no civil marriage or civil divorce, which means that it is impossible for mixed marriages to take place in Israel, at least between Jews and non-Jews. However, due to the obligations which Israel, like all other countries, is under in private international law, civil marriages and divorces contracted outside the state must be legally recognized, and any progeny is legitimate.

WHO IS A JEW? This is not the kind of problem that any other country has to deal with! The conflict between the constraints of religious law and the demands of modern life have been a major bone of contention in the Jewish community of Israel, but one to which there appears to be no immediate solution. The question of who is a Jew is a particularly vexed one, as the Jewish religious establishment in Israel refuses to recognize conversion to Judaism by non-orthodox communities in the Diaspora, such as the Progressive, Liberal and Reform movements of Europe and the United States. The 'Jewishness' of certain groups of Jews from remote parts of the world (in Jewish terms), such as the Beni Israel of India and the Falasha of Ethiopia, has also fallen under the suspicion of the rabbis in Israel.

There have, however, been some restraints applied to religious law, for instance, in the form of the Women's Equal Rights Law of 1951, which granted women equal status under law, overriding the precepts of Judaism and Islam.

Another problematic area of law inherited from the Ottomans is land law. This law is particularly complicated where a landowner dies intestate, because the land must be divided amongst all living relatives, even though his closest relatives – such as his widow and any young children – may need to realize the value of this land.

The laws – called ordinances in Palestine – passed by the British have generally been incorporated into Israeli law, including modification to property laws and especially company law. Criminal law has also remained largely British, although the death penalty was abolished almost immediately after the British left. The only exception to this rule is genocide. The only person to die for this crime has been Adolf Eichmann, hanged in 1962 after a famous trial.

Of course, the Knesset continues to pass new laws, and the

LEFT *The trial of Michael Dennis Rohan, who was convicted of having set fire to the El Aksa Mosque in 1969. Israel does not have jury trials; it has retained the judicial system of the British Mandate, whereby trial is by judge. In the case of the high and supreme courts, three and five judges sit, respectively. Jury trials would be impractical in an immigrant society where a member of the jury might favour a fellow countryman in the dock, regardless of guilt or innocence.*

BELOW *Tank captured from the Syrians, on the Golan Heights. Vast amounts of weapons were captured during the Six Day War in 1967, but virtually all are now obsolete.*

body of Israeli law enacted since 1948 contains some interesting innovations. One worthy of mention is the Statement of Reasons Law (Hok Ha-Hanmakot), under which a government official or civil servant refusing a petition from a member of the public must within six months provide a written explanation of why the request was refused.

THE ISRAEL DEFENCE FORCES

The institution which has excited the greatest admiration world-wide is the Israeli army. The reason for its success is twofold. One is that it is basically a standing army of civilians. All Israelis, men and women, must serve. The period of conscription has varied over the years, but at the time of writing it is three years for men, two for women. The only exemptions are deferments for university students, those studying at religious academies (*Yeshivot*) and married women. Israelis must spend one month in the army every year. This naturally causes great disruption to the economic life of the country. However, Israel is forced to spend a greater proportion of its gross national product on defence than any other country in the world, so this disruption is inevitable.

All food in the Israel Defence Forces is kosher, and Friday nights are celebrated in the traditional Jewish manner. Attendance at other prayers is optional.

The apparently lax attitude to discipline is deceptive. Israeli soldiers train with live ammunition, and manoeuvres are as arduous as they can be. Sadly, there is little need for spit and polish as a substitute for real combat, since there are constant battles to be fought, both large and small.

WOMEN IN THE ARMY

Although women can be classified medically as battle soldiers they are rarely called upon to serve in the front lines, though it has happened, especially in the 1973 War in Sinai. Not only is the Israeli woman soldier a symbol of 'the new Jew' and an object of envy throughout the world, but many other Third World countries (including Arab countries) have recruited women into the regular army. This would have been unthinkable had the Israelis not set the example. Israeli sociologists point to the presence of women as one of the reasons for the IDF's high morale. 'The Sabbath eve mess table laid with a white cloth, and the sight of a young girl soldier placing flowers on the cloth, is a greater morale booster than any pep talk I could ever give', says Major Avraham Tzivion, an army instructor.

Israel is about as classless a society as you can get, and the army reflects this fact. Soldiers are expected to salute their officers only once a day, if that. There are no separate messes for officers and men, though the officers' table is set apart. In any case, the pecking order becomes ridiculous when a young officer may in civilian life be a university student whose professor serves under him in the army as a sergeant or corporal.

ABOVE *Many women are employed as instructors in the Israel Defence Forces. An artillery instructor is showing new recruits how to operate tank weapons.*

RIGHT *Female tank crews undergoing training at army base camp. Although women fought in the front lines during the War of Independence, they were then relegated to the same sort of 'women's work' that female soldiers perform in every modern army. Thanks to feminist protests, the annotation 'battle soldier' on a woman soldier's medical profile is now beginning to mean just that.*

ABOVE *Colonel Ruth Muskal, one of Israel's most senior women officers. Women soldiers theoretically share equal duties with men, but in practice they are rarely put in the front line.*

LEFT *Israeli policewomen at a checkpoint inspecting an Arab car. This work is potentially dangerous, but there is no question of leaving it for the men to do.*

RIGHT *Israel's first Independence Day Parade, Jerusalem, 1949. It is seen passing the old Knesset building in King George Street, where Prime Minister Ben-Gurion and General Moshe Dayan are among those taking the salute.*

BELOW LEFT *Theodor Herzl, the founder of modern Zionism, sitting with members of the 5th Zionist Annual Congress held in Basle in 1901. Herzl is third from the left, second row from the bottom.*

BELOW *Aaron David Gordon (1856–1922), the Zionist philosopher behind the collective farming movement which led to the establishment of the kibbutzim and moshavim.*

THE STATE WITHIN A STATE

In 1948, the State of Israel was launched upon the world without any of the aid, assistance and encouragement now given to newly liberated countries as a matter of course by their erstwhile colonizers. It had no preset governmental structure, even the borders were not clearly defined, and it had to face a huge invading army from three sides.

The only reason Israel was able to fend off its attackers, and simultaneously form a sophisticated political structure which lasted for 40 years and more, was because this structure, including the army and police force, preceded the state.

The oldest of the frameworks on which the Jewish state came to be based is the World Zionist Organization, founded by Theodor Herzl himself in 1897. It has always been the main link between Israel and the Diaspora, fostering contacts, encouraging immigration and settlement and collecting funds.

Next came the Jewish National Fund, founded in 1901 with the object of purchasing land for the Jews to settle on. In addition to raising the vast amounts of capital required, the Jewish National Fund went on to do its own land reclamation work, a task in which it is still engaged today. The Jewish National Fund has planted over 150 million trees in areas laid waste by centuries of exploitation and neglect. It still prepares sites and builds roads. Land acquired in this way is never sold off to private individuals

but is always leased. The JNF and the state are by far the biggest landowners in Israel, and they own all the land on which the kibbutzim, moshavim and mitzpeh settlements are built.

Zionist activity in Palestine and abroad was given new impetus by the Balfour Declaration, a letter written in 1917 by Lord Balfour, then British foreign secretary, to Lord Rothschild, the unofficial leader of British Jewry. The letter stated that 'His Majesty's Government view with favour the establishment in Palestine of a national home for the Jewish people'. This unofficial, tentative and – as it turned out – temporary approval of Jewish settlement by the British government was a move to encourage this particular group of settlers. Other settler groups, the German Templars for instance, were openly hostile to the British victory in World War I and the subsequent mandate over Palestine.

Jewish organizations had always been concerned with the health of settlers in Palestine, and in raising health care standards in general. Many of the diseases endemic to the area – malaria, trachoma, tuberculosis – have only been completely eradicated in Israel since the establishment of the state. Three Jewish hospitals existed in Jerusalem by the early years of this century – Bikur Holim (est 1843), Misgav Ladach, a lying-in hospital (est 1888), and Shaare Zedek (est 1902). These hospitals still minister to the sick of all denominations, but all have new premises.

However, these hospitals were quite insufficient for the health needs of the country as a whole, and in 1912, an energetic Hungarian immigrant to the United States, Henrietta Szold, determined to found a health network to serve the entire Jewish community. The organization, which she called Hadassah, this being her own name in Hebrew, sent two trained nurses to work in Jerusalem in its first year of operation. From these modest beginnings sprung a network of preventive and public health services and a network of hospitals. The Hadassah Medical Centre was established with the Hebrew University in 1918 on Mount Scopus. The first nurses graduated from the School of Nursing in 1921.

After Mount Scopus became entirely cut off from Israel in 1948, Hadassah set about building a brand new medical centre in western Jerusalem. The Hadassah Medical Centre and School were opened in 1960 in Ein Karem, the suburb of Jerusalem which is incidentally also the village from which John the Baptist came. In addition to its magnificent medical facilities, the hospital synagogue houses the famous Chagall stained-glass windows depicting the Twelve Tribes. Thanks to the network of health care facilities offered by the Kupat Holim, other sick funds and the Ministry of Health, Hadassah can now concentrate more effort on vocational training. Perhaps its best-known venture in that field is the

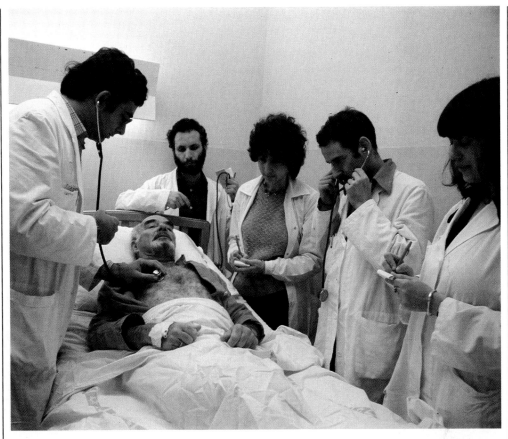

ABOVE *The consultant's visit, Hadassah-Hebrew University Medical Centre at Ein Karem. This magnificent complex was planned when the original medical centre on Mount Scopus was entirely cut off during the War of Independence in 1948, though technically it remained in Israel.*

RIGHT *The old Hadassah Medical School building at Mount Scopus has been restored since it again became accessible after the Six Day War in 1967. The nursing school is here once again, as it was in the days of Hadassah's founder, Henrietta Szold.*

· CHAIM WEIZMANN ·

Israel's first President, Chaim Weizmann (1874–1952), has been called 'the only truly Jewish statesman of the 20th century', as well as the 'first totally free Jew in the modern world'. Born in the White Russian village of Motol and raised in nearby Pinsk, the bright, middle-class Weizmann – the third of 12 children – studied chemistry at Darmstadt and Berlin in the early 1890s, eventually receiving his Ph.D. at Fribourg University in Switzerland. Later he lectured in organic chemistry in Geneva – his speciality was dye-stuffs – and in 1904 he began an association with Britain's Manchester University; it was here in 1906 he married Vera Chatzman (1882–1966), with whom he had carried on a 'passionate five-year correspondence'.

Since his Swiss student days, Weizmann had been active in Zionist groups, attending the Second Zionist Congress in 1898 and each subsequent one up to his death. His scientific pursuits coexisted with his Zionist activities throughout most of his long, busy life, which was marked by academic degrees and honours, as well as increasingly more significant roles in various Zionist groups. In 1908, Weizmann's first address to the Zionist Congress encouraged the combination of theoretical diplomacy with pragmatic settlement work in Palestine – a

school of thought later known as 'Synthetic Zionism'. His discovery of an important scientific method – that of synthesizing acetone, a solvent crucial to the production of munitions – led to a move to London in 1916 and a job with the Ministry of Defence. The move placed him in ever more powerful political circles, and he continued his tireless lobbying for a Jewish homeland. The next year, largely as a result of Weizmann's 'private campaign', the Balfour Declaration, wherein the British government recognized the quest for a Jewish

state, was signed. Weizmann – who had become a naturalized British subject in 1910 – was now 'the central figure in the public life of the Jewish people', laying the cornerstone of Hebrew University on Mount Scopus in Jerusalem (1919), being elected the President of the World Zionist Organization (1920), and travelling ceaselessly the world over to meet heads of state, both civil and crowned, in the name of Zionism. Revisionists assailed Weizmann's pro-British Zionism and in 1930 he resigned as head of the World Zionist Organization, but

five years later he was back at the helm, only to step down again in 1946 – a victim of near-blindness and the ascendancy of David Ben-Gurion. Despite his ill health and in-house political disagreements, in 1949 Weizmann was elected President of Israel, still an immensely popular figure, although politically a ceremonial figurehead; his memoirs, *Trial and Error*, were published the same year. He died in Rehovot, Israel, in 1952. Israel's famed Weizmann Institute of Science was named after this great statesman-scientist.

• DAVID BEN-GURION •

Twice Prime Minister of Israel, the fiery and charismatic David Ben-Gurion (1886–1973) was born David Gruen in Plonsk, north of Warsaw in Russian-ruled Poland. He was the sixth child of a lawyer/notary public; his mother had died when David was an infant. At the age of 20, David emigrated to Palestine, in defiance of his father's wishes. He worked as a farmhand and labourer in his new-found land, even choosing a new Hebrew surname around 1910, and ever tending the spark of Zionism which had been instilled in him as a boy, and which

had prompted him to leave Poland. He met his lifelong friend, Yitzhak Ben Zvi (second president of Israel) in Galilee, accompanying him to Salonika and Constantinople, but his zealous Zionism caused the Turks to expel him from all the lands in the Sultan's domain. During this time of 'expulsion', Ben-Gurion – at the time a member of the extreme left-wing *Poale Zion*, or Hebrew Social Democratic Party – went to America, along with Ben Zvi, to spread the Zionist creed, and in 1918 he met and married a New York nurse, Paula Munweiss, by whom he

was to have three children. Paula was pregnant with their firstborn, daughter Geula (meaning 'Salvation'),when Ben-Gurion temporarily abandoned her to join the Jewish Legion of the British army which was engaged in trying to free Palestine from Turkish rule.

By now an ardent non-Marxist socialist and bona-fide politician (though campaigning *for* a country, rather than in one), Ben-Gurion served as Secretary-General in the Jewish Labour Federation, the *Histadrut* (which mandated Palestine), and in 1930 became the head of the

Mapai, the Israel Workers party. He was Chairman of the Jewish Agency for Palestine from 1935 to 1948, this being the chief arm of the Jewish community during the British-mandate era. Upon proclamation of the Jewish state in 1948, Ben-Gurion declared himself its first Prime Minister, as well as Minister of Defence.

During both his tenures as Prime Minister (1948–53 and 1955–63), Ben-Gurion attempted to implement ambitious farming and industrial schemes throughout Israel. The Arab conflict was a deterrent in achieving all his enterprising goals, yet significant technological and agrarian advances were made under his aegis (he hated being referred to as a man 'in power'). After his resignation in 1963, Ben-Gurion went to the Kibbutz Sde-Boker in the Negev Desert, where he asked to be treated like all the other kibbutz members ('just David', he said, although a roster had referred to him as 'Mr Ben-Gurion'). A prolific writer of historical essays and personal remembrances, as well as a devotee of yoga, the revered elder statesman was living on the kibbutz when he died in 1973, and was duly honoured as a founding father of the State of Israel. Today among other things, a university and airport are name after David-Ben-Gurion, the 'saint of Israeli statehood'.

• THEODOR HERZL •

Theodor Herzl (1860–1904), the founder of modern Zionism, was born in Budapest, Hungary; after receiving a law degree in Vienna in 1884, he turned to a writing career. Although officially employed by a liberal Viennese newspaper from 1891 until his early death, he was known primarily as a freelance writer and playwright.

A four-year stint as a foreign correspondent in Paris made him acutely aware of that city's widespread anti-semitism – which was exacerbated by the notorious trial of Captain Alfred Dreyfus, a Jew falsely convicted of betraying France to Germany – and in 1896 Herzl published his major opus, *Der Judenstaat*, or *The Jewish State*, whose subtitle was 'An Attempt at a Modern Solution of the Jewish Question'. This was the first Zionist pamphlet to ever attract extensive attention, and in it Herzl proposed an orderly exodus of Jews to an as-yet-unknown region. Zionists had existed before Herzl, of course, but it was he who, with his dynamic, charismatic ways, transformed Zionism from a hodgepodge of inchoate, disparate feelings and groups into an organized, forceful and well-known entity – a true movement. This movement made its inaugural appearance at the First Zionist Congress in Basle, Switzerland, which Herzl convened in 1897, at the same time founding

the World Zionist Organization.

In his diaries, Herzl wrote that at Basle he had 'created the Jewish State', but in fact that concrete task was far from accomplished. Ever the diplomat, Herzl worked tirelessly towards this end – and towards his and many others' dream – meeting with political leaders and crowned heads of state throughout the

world, even securing an audience with Pope Pius X. Although some parties expressed interest and even posited possible locales – the Sinai, Cyprus and Uganda among them – all came to naught in Herzl's time, and disagreements among the Zionists ensued, with many deriding their leader for his futile, impractical diplomatic endeavours.

Nonetheless, when he died aged 44 – in part due to the intense physical strain he had worked under in the quest for his ultimate goal – the strong foundation for a Jewish state had been laid, with Theodor Herzl providing its cornerstone. Or to use a more appropriate metaphor, it was Herzl who had set the stage for the birth of modern Israel.

• MENAHEM BEGIN •

The fiery orator Menahem Begin was born in 1913 in Brest-Litovsk, in Tsarist-governed Poland, where he was taught at the *mizrachi* Hebrew schools and the Polish gymnasium, and where he later studied law at Warsaw University. Before the start of World War II, he played a significant role in the Polish Jewish Youth Movement, specifically the militant Betar group of Zionist-Revisionists, established by the Russian-Jew Vladimir Jabotinsky, a somewhat fanatical visionary whose dream of a reborn Jewish state became Begin's own vision. As the Germans advanced, Begin – by 1939 the head of the Polish Betar – fled eastward, was arrested in Vilna for 'anti-Soviet activity', and subsequently was incarcerated for a few months in 1940–41 in a Siberian concentration camp. Upon his release, in 1942 he went to Palestine, where he allied himself with an extreme Zionist faction, the *Irgun Zvai Leumi*, whose unofficial Commander-in-Chief he became (with an apparent bounty of £10,000 on his head). That same year he married Aliza Arnold, by whom he had three children.

In 1944 Begin ordered a revolt against the British mandate in Palestine, a bold action in blatant defiance of the official Zionist policy of cooperation with Britain against the Nazis. Begin went underground until the end of the war and the start of subsequent cooperation between the ruling Haganah leaders and the IZL, often cited as a 'very important landmark in [Begin's] career'. This bond broke down when in 1946 Begin decided to dynamite British army headquarters in the King David Hotel in Jerusalem. The British retaliated and the IZL was all but done away with,

but, phoenix as it was, it rose from the ashes to take part in the War of Independence. The IZL disbanded soon after Begin barely escaped death at the hands of Ben-Gurion, and its soldiers were taken into the newly established Israel Defence Forces, in the newly established State of Israel.

In place of the Irgun, the *Herut* (Freedom) movement was founded, with Begin at its helm; over the years, the party played a bigger and bigger role in Israeli politics, the former terrorist Begin himself metamorphosing into a respectable politician and statesman. In 1965, Begin's Herut joined forces with the Liberal party to become Gahal, and in 1973 Gahal fused with some small, right-wing parties to form the Likud. In 1977, the Likud became the ruling party, and from 1977 to 1983 its most renowned member, Menahem Begin, served as Prime Minister – this after nearly three decades of leading the loyal opposition in Israel's Parliament, the Knesset.

Begin's untiring quest for peace with the Arab world culminated in his historic meeting with Egyptian President Anwar Sadat at Camp David, Maryland, in September 1978, and the signing of the Israeli-Egyptian peace treaty, witnessed by US President Jimmy Carter. For their joint efforts, Begin and Sadat (who was assassinated in 1981) shared the 1978 Nobel Peace Prize.

In 1983 Begin shocked his colleagues and country by resigning, after a premiership which had lately been marked by a disheartening downward trend. He was succeeded by fellow Likud party-member Yitzhak Shamir, whose serves in that capacity today.

104

Hadassah School of Printing in Jerusalem, which has pioneered new modern Hebrew fonts, and made a valuable contribution to Hebrew typography.

The Jewish Agency was founded in 1929. It was basically the governing body of the Jewish community in Palestine, though not all the political streams were represented in it. Gradually, these came to be incorporated. The Jewish Agency ran the *Yishuv*, as the whole Jewish community in Palestine was called. It administered Jewish areas, paved roads, provided its own police and security service in the form of the *Ha-Shomer* (the Watchman Movement) and even had its own internal postal services. Other bodies such as the Alliance Israélite Universelle, a French organization, and the Jewish Colonization Association, founded by Baron Edmond de Rothschild, were taken over in 1924 by the Palestine Colonization Association (PICA). This was later to be called *Keren Ha-Yesod* (The Founding Fund), or the Joint Israel Appeal, the central administration fund for donations to Israel from Jews in the Diaspora. It was this money that kept the state going in the early years, when financial help from official sources outside Israel was non-existent; today, it still helps to back up the education system and medical services, hard hit as they are by defence spending.

The whole of this complicated structure, this 'state within a state', was run until 1948 by elected members representing the various Jewish communities called the *Asefat Nivharim* (Elected Assembly), set up in 1920. This assembly elected a body called the *Va'ad Ha-Leumi* (literally, the National Committee, which the British insisted on calling the General Committee, no doubt to avoid tacit admission of Jewish nationhood).

If the forerunner of the police was the Ha-Shomer movement, organized in 1909, the forerunner of the Israel Defence Army was the Haganah, founded in 1920. This secret organization smuggled weapons into kibbutzim and saved Israel from being destroyed in its infancy. The fighting arm of the Haganah, the Palmach, has become a byword for heroism in Israel. Both Ha-Shomer and the Haganah were formed to defend the Jewish settlers against Arab rioting, which the British did little or nothing to quell.

Just as importantly, in the same year that the Haganah was founded, so was the Histadrut (General Federation of Labour), Israel's equivalent of the Trades Union Congress or AFL–CIO. However, unlike the trades union umbrella organization in other countries, the Histadrut has parliamentary-style sessions at which elected delegates sit, and it owns and runs some important organizations such as Solel Boneh, Israel's biggest construction company, which also preceded the establishment of the state. The bus cooperative, Egged, and the dairy cooperative, Tnuva, were set up as

TOP *Israel introduced a national insurance scheme in 1954, one of the first developing countries to do so. Even with the problems of galloping inflation and an increasingly materialistic society, Israel is proud of the help and care it provides for the aged, the very young (Israel has a network of kindergartens which are unrivalled in the western world), and the disabled.*

ABOVE *Stamp commemorating the 100th anniversary of the birth of Henrietta Szold, the Hungarian-Jewish immigrant to the United States who founded the Hadassah women's movement. Hadassah is the Hebrew version of her name. In the background is a drawing of the Hadassah Medical Centre and School, which had then just opened at Ein Karem, on the outskirts of Jerusalem.*

part of the produce marketing strategy of the Jewish settlements long before independence was won. In 1980, Israel's equivalent of the Red Cross, the Red Shield of David (Magen David Adom) which provides paramedics and a nationwide ambulance service, celebrated its 50th anniversary. The Sick Fund clinics and most of the hospitals have their origins in the pre-state period. Incidentally, this is one reason why patients from all over the Middle East flock for health care to Israel, which has one of the longest life expectancies and lowest infant mortalities of any country in the world, as well as the highest doctor to patient ratios.

In many of its institutions of state, Israel superficially resembles any Western democracy. What makes it special is that Israel is not in the West. It is at the heart of the Middle East, surrounded by countries where to voice an anti-government opinion out loud, even among friends, can lead to imprisonment or even death, where executions are commonplace and the bodies are displayed with slogans attached to them for all the populace to see. Whatever the shortcomings – and they are many – the Israeli system grants a voice to everyone within its borders.

STRUCTURE OF THE ISRAELI STATE

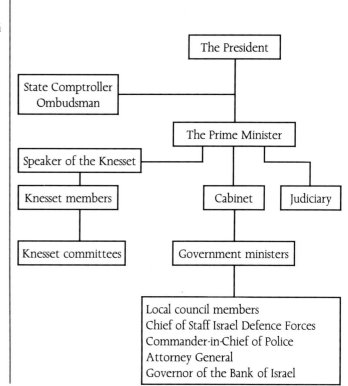

Chaim Weizmann 1949–1952

Yitzshak Ben-Zvi 1952–1963

Zalman Shazar 1963–1973

Ephraim Katzir 1973–1978

Yitzhak Navon 1978–1983

Chaim Herzog 1983–

THE PRESIDENTS OF ISRAEL

THE PEOPLE OF THE BOOK

LEFT *The kiosk, an important feature of every
Israeli town and village, which sells snacks,
cold drinks, cigarettes and, above all,
newspapers and magazines.*

ABOVE *Newspaper seller in Jerusalem. There are 15 daily papers in Hebrew, five in Arabic and nine in other languages. The Friday edition is the big weekend one, with lots of supplements and extra sections. News is vital in a country where the difference between war and peace may be the space of 24 hours, so copies are snapped up as soon as they appear.*

'Knowledge is like the sun – it dispells all darkness.'

YEHUDA LEIB GORDON

'Education is something which never ends.'

PROFESSOR ERNST SIMON

A RECENT UNESCO survey showed that Israelis read and publish more books per capita than any other people in the world. Over a million Israelis aged 14 and upwards read one book a month. About 1,000 books of Hebrew poetry and prose are published annually. It is not unusual for the print run of a poetry book to go as high as 3,000, exactly the same as it would be in a country of 70 million people such as Great Britain, or even of 220 million such as America. There are almost 100 Israeli publishers.

Israelis have a choice of 15 Hebrew daily newspapers reflecting all shades of political opinion, five newspapers in Arabic, and nine newspapers in foreign languages, including English – the *Jerusalem Post* was founded before the state as the *Palestine Post* – French, German, Russian, Hungarian, Polish, Romanian, Judezmo or Ladino (the Jewish language of the Sephardic Jews) and Yiddish. Israelis devour books; bookshops abound, and the Jerusalem International Book Fair, held every second year, is as thronged with visitors as the World's Fair in the United States or the Ideal Home Exhibition in Britain. Hebrew Book Week is an annual event, when the town squares are filled with stalls selling to an eager public.

Literacy has not been easily achieved. In many Jewish communities in the Diaspora, women were never educated unless

LEFT *Chayyim Nachman Bialik (1873–1934), considered to be the foremost modern poet in the Hebrew language. He was born in Volhynia, now in the USSR, and came to Israel in 1908.*

RIGHT *The bold, black letters of Hebrew shout out from every hoarding and street sign, evidence of the high literacy rate. Much emphasis has been placed on adult education, particularly among women from countries where female education is ignored.*

BELOW *Moroccan immigrants studying the Torah (the five books of Moses). Thanks to the age-old tradition of Jewish scholarship and the emphasis placed on learning, Jews are quick and anxious to acquire knowledge. This has made Jews from societies in which they were quite unused to the western way of life adapt amazingly quickly to their new lives in Israel.*

they were wealthy enough to afford private governesses. Among the Jews of Kurdistan, even the men were illiterate. It was a common sight at the post office in the 1950s and 1960s to see elderly people accepting delivery of a registered letter by placing their thumbprint on the receipt.

The Compulsory Education Law was passed in 1949 and now every Israeli citizen must attend school until the age of 14. Since 1978, education has been compulsory until 16 and free until the age of 18. Thirteen per cent of all Israelis receive higher education.

The Israel Defence Forces have been prime movers in the fight to achieve adult literacy. Especially in the periods of relative calm, soldiers have been sent to remote areas and development towns to live among Jewish immigrants from the Arab world and other parts of Asia and teach reading and writing in Hebrew. No one has ever been considered too old to learn.

There has been the additional – and far wider – problem of those who can read and write, but not in Hebrew. It has already been said that after independence, the population of Israel doubled in four years. How were all these people to be taught a new language – people from diverse cultural backgrounds, of all ages, families and single people, young and old? The answer was the *Ulpan*, an intensive Hebrew course lasting from three to six months, which is the envy of language teachers all over the world.

Ulpanim are run in towns as part of the absorption centres, so that the 'students' live on the premises, and on kibbutzim, where the 'students' learn in the morning and work in the afternoons. All of the teaching takes place in the Hebrew language, no matter how little knowledge the student has, because the class may consist of people of many different nationalities.

Participants from developing countries in Israel's aid program-

ISRAEL

HALBANON

1863 –

ABOVE *Yoel Moshe Solomon, printer and publisher of the first Hebrew newspaper in Palestine, Halbanon, which was published in 1863, about 20 years before the birth of modern Zionism. The newspaper was worded in the Hebrew style of the period, which now seems ludicrously quaint and old-fashioned; it only lasted for 12 issues, but was the forerunner of the modern Hebrew press.*

• THE HEBREW SCRIPT •

	OX	HOUSE
EGYPTIAN HIEROGLYPHICS *c*3000 BC		
CANAANITE *c*2000 BC		
PHOENICIAN *c*1000 BC		
HEBREW *c*700 BC		
OLD GREEK *c*650 BC		
ARAMAIC *c*350 BC		
FORMAL HEBREW *c*150 BC		
FORMAL GREEK *c*450 BC		
ROMAN *c*550 BC		

This table shows how modern Hebrew characters evolved simultaneously with Greek and Roman characters from a common prototype. Hebrew letters are called not by the sound they make but by the rough shapes they represent, which usually begin with the same letter of the alphabet. Thus the letter 'b', *bet*, means a house and the letter 'g', *gimmel*, means a camel. The printed Hebrew characters used today were originally developed by the

WATER	EYE	HEAD	PAPYRUS	
				Egyptian writing did not develop far from the use of pictorial symbols.
				Canaanite writing shows its pictorial origins, but in fact symbolizes basic sounds.
				The 22 basic symbols of the Canaanite system became the standard for the region.
				The Hebrews adopted the Canaanite alphabet in a modified form.
				The Canaanite origins can still be seen in archaic Greek script.
				Aramaic was the main language of the Persian Empire, and displaced Hebrew in Palestine.
				Classical Hebrew was written in a 'square' form of the common script of the region.
				The Greek alphabet allocated vowel sounds to some of the letters, and added more symbols.
				The Romans gained their alphabet from the Etruscans and Greek colonists.

OPPOSITE ABOVE *Ostracon (stone tablet) bearing the Hebrew inscription 'House of God' found in Arad, once the site of one of the minor Jewish Temples. It dates from the 6th century BC.*

OPPOSITE BELOW *Last columns of the Scroll of Isaiah, one of the Dead Sea Scrolls found in a cave in Qumran in the Judean Desert. The scroll contains Isaiah 65:4 to 66:24.*

Aramaic-speaking peoples to the north of Israel and were not adopted until the sixth century BC. Hebrew script characters are closer to older forms of Hebrew. Other forms of Hebrew script, the best known of which is the so-called Rashi script (after a famous rabbi who used it), have been used in the past. All are based on the proto-Canaanite alphabet. Different forms of Hebrew handwriting developed in isolated communities, such as those of Persia and Greece.

mes often attend these Hebrew classes so that later on they can get a better grasp of the techniques and skills of Israeli agriculture and industry. It is not an uncommon sight at ulpanim to see two African students who come from countries where different languages are spoken, conversing in Hebrew as their only common tongue. Israeli Arabs often speak Hebrew to each other when they go abroad if they don't want other Arabs to understand what they are saying!

The choice of Hebrew as the national language of Israel has been a tremendous unifying force. Almost every Jewish community outside Israel has its own jargon, which in some cases, such as Yiddish and Judezmo (Ladino or Judaeo-Espagnol), has developed into a rich language with its own literature and culture. However, each of these languages is peculiar to a different section of Jewry. Only Hebrew, the language of prayer, unites all Jews.

Hebrew, for so long a dead language, the language only of liturgy, is one of the oldest living tongues. Inscriptions in Proto-Canaanite script, one of the forerunners of Hebrew script, have been found in Israel which date from the 12th century BC, and this makes them older than either Chinese or Greek. The script used today was introduced as early as the 6th century BC.

The revival of Hebrew and its development into a modern language containing concepts such as 'data-processing' (*ibud netunim*), 'escalation' (*haslama*) and 'design' (*itzuv*) is due almost entirely to the efforts of one man. Eliezer Ben-Yehuda (1858–1922) was born Eliezer Isaac Perelmann. He emigrated to Palestine from Lithuania in 1881, and soon came to realize that a single unifying language was needed for the Jews in Palestine, a few of whom already spoke Hebrew to each other (with the Sephardic pronunciation which is now standard in modern Hebrew) but most of whom spoke Judezmo or Yiddish. Ben-Yehuda decided to strive to make Hebrew the national language. He started in his own home; his son, Itamar Ben-Avi, has written much of how he was brought up as the first child for more than a thousand years whose mother tongue was Hebrew.

Others soon rallied to Ben-Yehuda's side, and in 1920 he founded the Hebrew Language Academy, the Vaad Ha-lashon Ha-Ivri. The Academy still acts as the arbiter of new Hebrew words, though its proposals are not always adopted into common speech. The teaching of Hebrew outside the Diaspora has undergone a great revival, led from Israel by the Council of the Teaching of Hebrew, based in Jerusalem.

Hebrew has also spawned a rich literature, one that has been more frequently translated into English than that of any other language with a comparable number of speakers (only about six

RIGHT *Eliezer Ben-Yehuda (1858–1922) pioneered the revival of Hebrew and its development into a modern language. He founded the Hebrew Language Academy in 1920, which still acts as the arbiter of new Hebrew words.*

ABOVE *Stamp commemorating the second annual Jerusalem International Book Fair. The Fair was first held in 1963, and was an enormous success. It is held every second year, and grows bigger and bigger every time. During the fair, the Jerusalem Prize for Literature is awarded to an author of international status. In recent years, since the peace agreement with Egypt, Egyptian and even Lebanese publishers have exhibited at the fair.*

million worldwide). As Israel declared statehood only in 1948, any literature prior to that date is technically non-Israeli. In practice, however, May 1948 is not a particularly significant watershed. The official language of the new state was to be Hebrew, and Israeli literature inherited the long tradition of Hebrew literature, whose origins are biblical and whose written output extended over several millennia and to all parts of the world where Jewish communities and culture flourished.

More specifically, Israeli literature takes up the tradition of the Hebrew literature of modern times, bringing together two major trends: the secularizing, although partially nationalist, tendency of the Jewish Enlightenment (from the late 18th century onwards) and the tendency towards a return to the homeland of the land of Israel where the culture could flourish unhampered. The Hebrew literature of the Enlightenment struggled for increased lexical and syntactic scope and for an extension of literary genres beyond the medieval and traditionalist confines. A breakdown of the old communal and religious structures in the wake of secularization and social unrest was noted by the new Hebrew writers, sometimes with enthusiasm and sometimes with foreboding. In the late 19th century, satirists such as the Yiddish and Hebrew novelist, Mendele Mokher Sforim (1836–1917), both attacked characteristic social patterns and mourned the passing of the old. The leading Hebrew poet of his time, Chayim Nachman Bialik (1873–1934), blended his own sense of existential tragedy with a description of the national character of the Jewish people to create the effects of an ineradicable pathos.

Prior to World War I, the chief centres of modern Hebrew creativity were to be found in the Diaspora, particularly in eastern Europe. But the ravages of that war, the Bolshevik revolution and the Russian civil war effectively destroyed the old-style Pale of Settlement and the shtetl from within. This process was to be completed during World War II and the destruction of European Jewry. Meanwhile, the British victory in World War I, following the British offer of a homeland to the Jewish people, enshrined in the Balfour Declaration of November 1917, stimulated the movement of Jews to what was then Palestine. The wave of Jewish immigration (the third such wave in the post-war period) more than doubled existing Jewish settlement. Despite major setbacks, the *Yishuv* (the Jewish community in Palestine) established itself as an autonomous entity – a state in the making. The systematic persecution of European Jewry in the period between the world wars reinforced this tendency, so that by 1939 a state could begin to emerge, though it was constantly challenged by Arab opposition.

After World War II, the centres of Hebrew creativity were dead or dying in three major areas: in western Europe, where the Holocaust had trapped the Jews and destroyed their culture; in eastern Europe, where those Jews who survived the Holocaust found that Communism was throttling the 'counter-revolutionary' language of Hebrew, together with other independent sources of Jewish expression; and in the United States (which had become the home of the single largest Jewish population in the world), where cultural and linguistic assimilation proceeding apace. In the new circumstances, the only possible centre for Hebrew was Palestine/Israel.

With Israeli independence Hebrew could now flourish, not just as a literary language but as a current vernacular and the official medium of expression of the new state. In the early 1900s Hebrew writers had established themselves in Palestine, so that by the 1920s a self-conscious Palestinian-Hebrew literature had been created. Avraham Shlonsky (1900–1973), Uri Zvi Greenberg (1896–1983) and Nathan Alterman (1910–1970), all poets whose talents were rooted in eastern Europe, moved to Palestine in this period.

ABOVE *Natan Alterman (1910–1970), a Hebrew poet much of whose work has been set to music, like that of Uri Zvi Greenberg.*

LEFT *Uri Zvi Greenberg (1896–1983), another Hebrew poet of Russian origin, whose lyric poetry and simple style are of particular appeal to the modern reader.*

BELOW *Yehuda Amichai (b 1924), poet and novelist, sitting outside his new home in the Jewish Quarter of the Old City of Jerusalem, with Mount Zion in the background.*

114

Abba Kovner (1918–1987), a poet and philosopher, was instrumental in the concept and planning of the Museum of the Diaspora in Ramat-Aviv. He was a leader of the partisans in the Vilna Ghetto during the Holocaust, and settled in Israel after World War II.

FAR RIGHT *Rachel Blumstein (1890–1931), a Russian-born Israeli poetess and member of Kibbutz Kinneret, much of whose work has been set to music. She died of tuberculosis.*

OPPOSITE *S Y Agnon (1888–1970), the modern Hebrew novelist and poet, and the only major modern Israeli writer to adhere to traditional Jewish religious orthodoxy. He was joint winner of the Nobel Prize for Literature (with the Swedish-Jewish poetess, Nelly Sachs) in 1966.*

S Y Agnon (1888–1970) returned to Palestine in 1924 after an earlier stay there before World War I. He is the best-known Hebrew writer outside Israel, having shared the Nobel Prize for Literature in 1966 with the Swedish poet (and Holocaust survivor), Nelly Sachs. The Oriental Hebrew novelist Yehuda Burla (1887–1969) was Palestinian-born, as was the poet, Esther Raab (1899–1980). These writers drew their inspiration from their native soil.

Some of the immigrant writers, sought in different ways, to assume a Palestinian identity by obliterating traces of the Jewish Diaspora. Yosef Chaim Brenner (1881–1921) had warned against adopting a 'Palestinian genre', and this might have influenced the writers of the second wave starting in 1909, but the third wave established a specifically Palestinian local literature. In 'Matzada', 1927, a long poem by Yitzhak Lamdan (1900–1954), the poet-narrator idealized labour in the style of a Russian revolutionary poet. Greenberg had a prophetic bent, and Agnon turned to the Palestinian epic. Chayim Hazzaz (1898–1972) incorporated the Palestinian scene into his narrative subject matter.

By 1948 a Hebrew literature based in the Land of Israel, the Jewish milieu in Palestine, had evolved contemporaneously with a highly developed social and political structure. Some of the notable exponents of Israeli literature had begun writing before the establishment of the state. The sabra novelist, Yizhar Smilansky (b 1916), began to publish in 1938, seeking, in what was still a language lacking in many modern concepts, a richer lexical and syntactic language for the narrative. However long the story, the plot in Smilansky's work is always sparse. His central concerns are the landscape, the moral issue, the indecisive hero and the language itself – the plot is unresolved by any action. The poetry of Chayim Guri (b 1921), which started to appear at the close of the War of Independence, focuses on the fighting, the hero, his beloved and his gory memories – a very local scene. Many of the heroes in the novels and stories of Moshe Shamir (b 1921) are not only native-born, but see themselves as a different breed from the Diaspora Jew. The new Israeli is characterized as simple, direct, active, healthy, single-minded and strong, in contrast to the town-dwelling, cringing, tortured Diaspora Jew of Europe. Shamir also founded a small periodical, *Yalkut Ha-Re'im*, whose style is referred to as

'Palmach literature', referring to the Palmach, the combat arm of the pre-state Jewish fighting force, the Haganah. The subject matter was, in general, emergent Israel: absorption of immigrants, the war, the kibbutz, the issues of the new state. The concerns were practical and ideological, collective rather than individual.

The 1950s witnessed changes on various fronts. Poets became more introspective and sceptical, dubious about socialist idealism and ideology. They began uncertainly to look over their shoulders to their forebears and an earlier Jewish existence. Yehuda Amichai (b 1924) makes much of the contrast between the generations, a theme highlighted by the unexpected image become metaphor. Amir Gilboa (1917–1986), whose initial power derives its original expression from the Jewish predicament and Israeli independence, articulated uncertain introspection in his later poetry. Natan Zach (b 1930) has always been concerned with the private world of the poet and the delicate structure of interpersonal relationships. Pinchas Sadeh (b 1929), seeing life as a parable (his book of that name was published in English in 1971), started to produce a rather un-Israeli type of confessional prose, whose concerns were the self, truth and God.

Intense religious experience has not featured prominently amongst Israeli authors, although the poet Zelda (1913–1985) expressed an ecstatic certainty of God's presence in the face of death. But away from public commitments, the heroes of Israeli novels of the 1950s and 1960s are seen in flight from their official or imagined roles. Shamir's work has moved in this direction, just as he has moved from the extreme left to the extreme right politically, as he has aged. The characters of the novelist, Aharon Megged (b 1920), are sometimes disillusioned, making their way from the kibbutz to the city, as in *Chedvah va'Ani* (*Chedvah and I*) of 1954, or away from enslavement to the national myth, as in *Ha-Chay al Ha-Met*, 1965 (*The Living on the Dead*, translated into English and published in 1970).

Israeli existence was, of course, multi-faceted. But ideologies had not only been promoted as necessary during the constant conflict, they were sometimes portrayed as being peculiar and exclusive to the new Israel. One such ideology was aired in the periodical, *Alef*, founded in the 1940s to advocate a sort of Hebrew–pan-Semitic Union, a Middle Eastern Jewish state, but one linked more closely to its neighbours, and isolated from Diaspora Jewry. Another, although less clear-cut, ideology appeared in a forum entitled *Likrat*, distributed from 1952 onwards; this had neither a leftist nor rightist orientation. These were alternative voices to the prevailing Zionist line, but these voices were often muted as the literature of Israel became less sure of itself and its

ABOVE *The Technion, Israel's first technical university, which has been the model for many similar institutions in the developing countries, was founded in 1924 and immediately became the subject of controversy. The German-Jewish charity, the Hilfsverein, which had sponsored the foundation, wanted the language of instruction to be German. The students insisted on using Hebrew for their studies and went on strike until they got their way!*

direction less certain. Israel was and is characterized by divisions of the type experienced by other democracies. Its people are becoming increasingly concerned with their own situation. So too has its literature become less publicly oriented, although the Land of Israel remains, at least subliminally, its subject.

One aspect of the revival of Israel in the context of Hebrew literature is the emergence of drama, the Cinderella of literary genres, into the limelight. Hebrew drama had always been relatively weak, for lack of a living vernacular, for lack of a stage and for lack of a Hebrew tradition in the genre (though the same was not true of Yiddish theatre in Russia and Poland). But Nissim Aloni (b 1926), who had written naturalistically of his youth in his fiction, turned to poetic fantasies in his plays. Perhaps this removal from current reality illustrates a difficulty of Hebrew drama. Hanoch Levin (b 1943), on the other hand, is a satirist, whose characters parody Israeli obsessions and political and social attitudes. At first execrated by the general public as unpatriotic, particularly with the staging of *Malkat Ha-Ambatyah*, 1972 (*Queen of the Bathtub*) a searing attack on the premiership of Golda Meir, Levin is now in

the mainstream of Israeli drama. His hero bases his life on expectation rather than fulfilment, and so enlightens the public on the nature of human aspirations. Yehoshua Sobol (b 1939) uses historical events to focus on the moral issues in his plays.

More recent years have seen Hebrew literature dwell on the past, Jewish history formative of the present, and on the future. Aharon Appelfeld (b 1932), a Holocaust survivor from Tchernowitz, Romania, writes mainly of European Jewry in its twilight world, reaching for assimilation on its path to destruction, and of the world of the survivors rooted in that past. It is both the world of the author's childhood and the public Israeli world of an often unacknowledged infancy. The novelist, A B Yehoshua (b 1937), has stated that his object is to portray contemporary Israeli man and his paradoxical dilemmas. Amos Oz (b 1939) has sought symbols of the Israeli situation, images of terror and siege that haunt ordinary people, whose interior lives are really quite extraordinary. Both Appelfeld and Oz are well known to the English-speaking world through translations of their work.

Many of Israel's younger fiction writers view Israel within a larger context; either in its state of constant terror and siege or in relation to a past which still coexists with the present. The current scene abounds with experimentation in mimesis. Amalia Kahana-Carmon (b 1926) has long been writing intensely rendered stream-of-consciousness stories, often as if they were narrated by a child or by an adult with a childlike point of view who is fixated on another individual. Yaakov Shabtai (1934–1982) produced a series of short narrative extravaganzas, then a long novel, composed of a single paragraph, *Zikhron Dvarim*, 1977 (translated into English as *Past Continuous*, 1985), moving from one death at its opening to another at its close: first the father's, then the son's, a suicide. His unfinished novel, *Sof Davar*, (*Past Perfect*), 1987 was published posthumously, and marks new experimentational paths for the Hebrew novel.

A very complex picture emerges in a survey of the modern Israeli literary scene. The dominant language is now Hebrew, although literature in other languages is produced, notably in Arabic by Arabs living in Israel. There are many Arab poets, such as Samih Al-Qassem, Mahmoud Darwish and Tawfiq Zayid, who write bitter poems of protest against what they see as their position in Israeli society. Many of these writers, including Emil Habibi, a Communist member of the Knesset, are strongly left wing.

Muhammed Ali Taha is a writer of novels and short stories, one of whose best-known novels, *Aid Al-Miari*, (1978), is about the massacre of Palestinian Arabs by the Lebanese Phalangists in the refugee camp of Tel Za'atar outside Beirut in 1978. Ahmed Hussein, a poet and short-story writer, is another who focuses on the Palestinian cause.

Serious drama is a new medium for Middle Eastern writers in Arabic, but they have produced some important works, such as *An-Natour* by Salim Makhuli, 1979, about land expropriated by Arabs for Jewish settlement.

Jewish writers whose mother tongue is English have made a serious contribution to Israeli literature. Most noteworthy is T Carmi, who was born in New York, but is one of the best-known Hebrew poets. Dennis Silk is a poet who writes in English, and there are novelists such as Lesley Hazleton, Lionel Davidson and Yael Dayan whose works are produced in English. Of the expatriate American writers who have settled in Israel, the best known is probably Ira Levin (author of *Rosemary's Baby* and *The Stepford Wives*, among others), who has made his home in Herzliya Pituah, an attractive seaside town north of Tel-Aviv.

Hebrew is a language rich in religious and liturgical concepts, but young as a vernacular. Its writers cover only a few generations but hail from vastly diverse cultural and geographical back-grounds. But they jostle together in the turbulent current of Hebrew literature; the young and the old, the Israeli-born and the immigrant, the Zionist conservative and the radical, the Oriental and the European Jew, the religious and the secular, the hopeful and the disillusioned. Fortunately the interest in Hebrew and Israel, combined with a large body of competent translations, has brought Hebrew literature, if only in translation, to a wide audience outside Israel.

ABOVE *Raymonda Hawa Tawil (b 1940), a Christian Arab writer from the West Bank whose works of protest have been published in Israel in both Hebrew and Arabic. Her book,* My People, My Prison, *has been translated into English.*

LEFT *Amos Oz (b 1939), the Jewish Israeli novelist, is well known to the English speaking world through translations of his work.*

ISRAEL AT WORK

LEFT *Scientist using an electron microscope at the Haifa Technion, Israel's oldest technical university and one of the first such institutions in the world. Israel is a recognized world leader in high technology.*

'Whatever thy hand findeth to do, do it with all
thy might.'

ECCLESIASTES 9:10

ISRAEL CAN FAIRLY be described as the Japan of the Middle East, the most heavily industrialized country in the region, with a style and originality to its products which rival those of the larger industrialized nations.

Why this should be is best summed up in a favourite Israeli phrase: *ayn brera*, 'there is no alternative'. Israel has very few natural resources – not enough oil for its own needs, some potash, nitrates and a little copper. There is no coal or natural gas, and no other minerals, precious metals or precious gemstones. The only other resources are sulphur, bitumen and manganese.

Add to this the fact that this tiny strip of land is half desert and has a 90 per cent urban population, and you can see why there has been an urgent need to industrialize. As if this were not enough, there are the huge proportion of the budget spent on defence and the need to spend on social programmes such as immigrant absorption (Israel has a welfare state on European lines). In the early years of the state imports had to be cut to a minimum and exporting was a dire necessity. There were also the pressures of the Arab boycott to consider, which were once extremely onerous but have become less and less effective, to the extent that there is now a flourishing clandestine (on both sides) trade with the Arab world.

Almost 25 per cent of the population is employed in industry, and manufacturing accounts for 20 per cent of the gross national product. The kibbutzim make a major contribution to Israel's industrialization. Starting with a few knitting and plastics factories in the early 1960s, the 330 kibbutz factories now account for 5 per cent of Israel's total industrial output and 6 per cent of exports (excluding diamonds).

The lack of raw materials has led Israel to concentrate on manufactured products with high added values, putting to best advantage the only natural asset Israel has – the skills of her people. Of the refugees who came to Israel from central Europe in the 1920s, 1930s and 1940s, some possessed rare and invaluable skills, such as glassmaking, diamond-cutting, jewellery-making and fine engraving. Their efforts were put into the founding of the Phinikia Glassworks, a major exporter of window glass and other industrial and construction glassware, the diamond and jewellery industry, the printing industry and other skilled trades. Their skills

RIGHT *Oron Phosphate Works, near the Dead Sea. Phosphates and nitrates, used mainly to make artificial fertilizers and explosives, are Israel's only significant natural resources.*

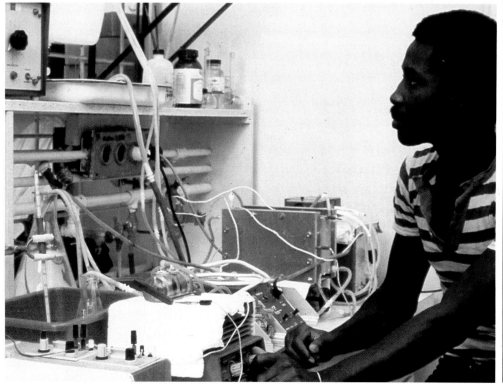

have been supplemented by highly trained immigrants from western Europe and lately from Poland and Russia. Native-born Israelis receive excellent training for industry in the education network, ranging from vocational schools at the high-school level to institutions of higher education such as the Haifa Technion–Institute of Technology and the postgraduate Weizmann Institute. The Weizmann Institute is named after the first president of the State of Israel, Dr Chaim Weizmann, himself a scientist of note. A second scientist, Dr Ephraim Katzir, a nuclear physicist, was president of the State of Israel from 1974 to 1979. Since the presidency is an honorary role, this shows how highly esteemed science is in Israel. In fact, one of the greatest scientists of all time, Albert Einstein, was offered the presidency in 1948, but he declined due to pressure of work.

One of Israel's major exports consists of processing a raw material which is entirely imported. The Diamond Exchange in Ramat-Gan, just north of Tel-Aviv, was one of the first tower blocks in the country, whose elaborate security system has been the subject of at least one thriller film. Israel's diamond industry produces about 80 per cent of the world output of small polished gemstones. It is also responsible for 40 per cent of diamond polishing of all types, and it is thus the largest processor and marketer of cut diamonds in the world. There are even kibbutz factories engaged in diamond-polishing, but most of the work is done by small workshops in Tel-Aviv, Ramat-Gan and Netanya.

Research and development of high technology are so important to Israel that even with its limited resources and the enormous demands on the budget, the country spends even more on basic research than West Germany and Japan, and almost as much on applied research as the United States. Metals, machinery and

OPPOSITE LEFT *A research laboratory at the Weizmann Institute, the oldest of Israel's many research establishments. Israel's greatest resources are its manpower and the brainpower of its people.*

OPPOSITE TOP RIGHT *Israelis polishing diamonds. Despite the fact that not a single diamond is found in the country, Israel has become the number-one diamond polishing and processing centre of the world. Polished diamonds are Israel's leading industrial export, and bring in more revenue than citrus fruit.*

OPPOSITE BELOW *An African scientist working at the Weizmann Institute. Israel has a massive foreign aid programme, the largest of any country of its size in the world. The aid is not merely financial, but also consists of teaching and further education for people from developing nations in Asia and Africa.*

RIGHT *The Dead Sea Works, a major industry that was founded before the establishment of the state. Today, specially designed plastic piping, coloured to indicate the type of liquid flowing through it, is used to carry the highly corrosive Dead Sea chemicals.*

RIGHT *An offshore oil platform near Eilat. Israel's only landbased oilfield is in Heletz, near the Gaza Strip, and despite constant exploration, no further oil has been found. Exploration on- and offshore continues, since Israel, as the most highly industrialized country in the region, is also the area's largest consumer per capita of petroleum products.*

LEFT *Laser research at the Weizmann Institute. Israelis have been in the forefront of discovering and developing new uses for laser beams, in everything from weaponry to surgery.*

RIGHT *Particle accelerator at Beer-Sheba's University of the Negev. It is hardly surprising that Israel has a particular interest in nuclear physics, since Albert Einstein was an ardent Zionist, who was once offered the presidency of the State of Israel. Former president Ephraim Katzir is also a nuclear scientist.*

LEFT *Aerial view of the Hebrew University campus at Givat Ram on the western side of the city. When the Mount Scopus campus was abandoned, the university again functioned from temporary quarters until these buildings were opened in 1952, on the western side of the city. The sentimental Jerusalem bus cooperative, Ha-Mekasher, reserved the number 9 for the bus route that had run to Mount Scopus, and after the Six Day War, the number 9 bus ran once more, this time linking the two campuses.*

electronics are Israel's biggest exports, and its computer products are used in almost every country in the world. Inside Israel, robotics has revolutionized factory working. Among the most successful high-tech developments are the tomograph, a body scanner that makes cross-sectional X-rays, lasers with industrial and medical applications, the Westwind and Astra executive jet planes, and the Scitex, a computerized colour-printing machine that is used to reproduce the colour photographs in the world's leading magazines, such as *Time* in the United States and internationally.

The Judaean Hills are sometimes known to industrialists as Israel's 'silicon hills', where small firms of developers work busily away at creating software and equipment for the world's major computer companies, most of it anonymously. The big hardware multinationals are well aware of the inventiveness and creative ability of the Israelis, and take full advantage of it.

Enormous effort has been put into solving Israel's twin major long-term problems, lack of fossil fuels and lack of water. The sun's rays were harnessed to produce energy at an early stage. Israeli homes had solar water heaters at least 20 years before anyone else, and Israel is now the world leader in the technology. In addition to heating one-quarter of Israeli homes, solar energy is being used in Israel to heat hospitals and factories. A novel use for solar energy is to run air-conditioning plants, obviously the most practical use as cooling is needed most when the sun's energy is highest. In 1983, the first solar power station was built on the shores of the Dead Sea, and it is the first of several. The power stations can operate continuously, because they store the sun's rays in a series of shallow high-saline pools.

Desalination plants are another area in which Israel is a world leader. The first commercial plant was built on the Red Sea in Eilat. Every other device imaginable has been used to increase the

ABOVE *Haifa University has expanded greatly in recent years, and occupies a campus on the northwestern slopes of Mount Carmel.*

ABOVE RIGHT *The Bee Research Centre at the Hebrew University's Agriculture Department in Rehovot. Commercial beekeeping in Israel was begun by a British expert who went to live on Kibbutz Erez, near the Gaza Strip, in 1948.*

available amount of water, including cloud-seeding.

The same ingenuity has been applied over the years to the lifestyles of Israel's own citizens. Israel is full of *patentim* – clever ideas. The brightly coloured vertical and horizontal louvred blinds enclosing balconies which are such a feature of housing in Tel-Aviv and the coastal plain are an Israeli invention which other hot countries would do well to adopt. The fibreglass and plastic materials keep the balconies cool and aired, and prevent the heat from being trapped and even increased as do the glassed-in balconies of the Arab world. Israeli cosmetics and detergents have benefited from the boycott, in that the homegrown industry had time to get started before the big multinationals moved in. Again,

the quality is superior to much of what one can buy in Europe and America, and prices are lower. One range of skin-care products is based on Dead Sea minerals, including a mud pack. Telma, the processed-food company, recently discovered that its cosmetic hair-removal pad, which uses a brand-new technique, was earning it more export dollars than its food products.

Ingenious kitchen gadgets have been invented to cope with the Israeli lifestyle. In addition to universally handy items such as an olive/cherry-pitter cum garlic press cum can-opener, and a cake knife with two prongs so the cake can be picked up on the knife end for serving, there are the wonderpot and the frying-pan-style grillpan, already mentioned elsewhere in this book, and a device for roasting chickens vertically in cramped oven space. There are also ovens which fit over a gas ring. Foam-producing scouring pads and dish detergent which comes in a block are designed to use a minimum of precious water when cleaning dishes.

These are some of Israel's 'small' ideas. By far the biggest Israeli idea is drip-feed irrigation. This device threatens to revolutionize desert agriculture; Israeli drip-feed systems, supervised and run by Israelis, have been installed in all the arid regions of the world from El Centro, California, to Timbuctoo, Mali, a total of 47 countries so far. The company that produces the systems, Netafim, is a joint venture of three kibbutzim, Hatzerim, Magal and Yiftah, as widely separated geographically as is possible in Israel. Kibbutz

ABOVE *Irrigation pipes, pumping water to a drip-feed system. The red pipes hold sea water, the blue, fresh water. The mixture is fed to the plants and produces surprisingly good crops. In tomatoes, for instance, the salt stimulates the plant to produce more sugars, making the tomatoes particularly sweet.*

RIGHT *The kibbutzim have been in the forefront of developing new techniques for producing flowers in winter for the European market. This greenhouse is at Kibbutz Gilat.*

Hatzerim is in the Negev Desert, Magal is in the fertile Hefer Valley on the coastal plain, and Yiftah is in Galilee.

The drip-feed irrigation system works by pumping plant nutrients dissolved in water through plastic piping perforated with minute holes, beneath each of which a seedling is planted. Each seedling receives just the right amount of water and nutrients fed in droplets through the perforations. In this way, not a drop of water is wasted in the surrounding soil; all the nourishment goes to feed the crops.

In addition to this and other agricultural machinery, such as a multi-purpose tractor, Israel's agricultural exports are still the second-biggest dollar-earner. Israeli citrus products, especially the famous Jaffa oranges, known technically as the shamouti, are a byword. In the early years of the state and in the pre-state period, the oranges were almost the only big export crop.

However, today's enormous export market in Israeli fruits and vegetables is the product of much behind-the-scenes hard work in agricultural research and marketing. Israel introduced the avocado to Europe, and it had a hard time persuading European sellers and housewives that an avocado pear was not a kind of dessert pear! Chinese leaves (Chinese cabbage) were also popularized in Europe by the Israelis, as was the pomelo, a kind of giant grapefruit with a slightly milder flavour. The biggest success story was a strain of Persian melon that was sweeter and more delicate in flavour than

hitherto known, and developed at Kibbutz Ha-Ogen. Ogen melons proved to be too successful; the Spanish found the seeds were fertile and began growing them themselves, thus grabbing a large part of Israel's export market.

Irrigation and water conservation are a major preoccupation. Slogans and signs everywhere urge Israelis to conserve water, a far more precious commodity in the Middle East than oil. Research is proceeding apace to see how much food can be produced using brackish and saline water. Even fish-farming is using recycled water. Carp, a favourite fish for the eastern European dish of gefilte fish (ground fish), is farmed in ponds in northern Israel and the Beth Shean Valley. Tillapia and gilthead bream, both fish found in the

ABOVE A familiar sight at dawn and dusk is the spray from the irrigation pipes. Most of Israeli agriculture is under irrigation. The National Water Carrier, a complex system of pipes, uses the Jordan waters to distribute water throughout the country.

RIGHT These onions are being grown in 30 per cent brackish water. More and more crops are being grown in saline or partly saline water, with ever greater success.

ASPECTS OF ISRAELI AGRICULTURE

The search for new crops which Israel can produce more economically than elsewhere and sell for export is a continuing process. It is no exaggeration to say that Israel puts more money and effort into crop research than any other country in the world. Almost every tropical and sub-tropical crop has been experimented with, including coffee and pistachio nuts – two that didn't make it! Two fruits from Israel that may soon be seen in the shops are the pitanga or Brazilian cherry and the acerola or Barbados cherry. The latter is the richest source of vitamin C occurring in nature and is already being produced for Israel's important pharmaceutical industry.

In the 1960s and 1970s, Israel's agricultural economy grew by an average of 12 per cent per year, the fastest-growing in the world, although it has now slowed somewhat. Israel is largely self-sufficient in food, and has the highest yield per acre (or per dunam, the Israeli measure of land equivalent to a quarter of an acre) of wheat of any country in the world. This is made possible because the mild Israeli climate enables the sowing of three crops per year, two of which are irrigated.

ABOVE RIGHT *Pistachio trees growing near Avdat, in the northern Negev. So far, these trees have grown only in the cooler, mountainous areas of Lebanon and Iran. If they can be persuaded to produce their valuable crop of nuts in this harsher climate, they will be a valuable addition to the range of Israeli produce. Similar experiments have been conducted in coffee-growing.*

RIGHT *Globe artichokes, which are native to the area, grow on a thorny bush. They are members of the thistle family.*

LEFT *This complicated piece of agricultural machinery was invented in Israel for picking peppers. Red and green peppers are an important feature of the Israeli diet, as well as a valuable export crop.*

FAR LEFT *Old-fashioned agriculture still exists in Israel and is practised almost exclusively by the Arabs. This Arab farmer is ploughing in the time-honoured way, using a donkey and a wooden plough, in the stony soil of Galilee. Almost all Arab farmers have tractors, but some prefer the old methods.*

Great Bitter Lake, a part of the Suez Canal, are being farmed in Israel using brackish waters, with excellent results. Shrimp farming is another successful fish-farming venture. Since shrimp are not kosher (that is, do not conform to Jewish dietary laws), almost all the shrimp are exported.

The processed-food industry is a natural byproduct of Israel's prolific agriculture. It is one of the most highly automated and sophisticated in the world, but the need to employ special supervisors to ensure that Israeli foods meet the strict requirements of Jewish dietary laws has sometimes made them uncompetitive in world markets. However, they have a ready market in Jewish food stores throughout the world, and their superior quality makes them an important export. In addition to packaged soups, quick-setting vegetarian jelly (gelatin), noodles and other dry products, kosher dairy products are now reaching Europe in the form of margarine, low-fat cheeses and yoghurt. The Tival company markets a range of vegetarian meat substitutes such as vegetarian

sausage rolls and vegetarian breaded cutlets which can be found in health food stores and some supermarkets throughout the western world.

Israel's expertise in agriculture and food processing has been invaluable to the third world. In the 1950s and 1960s, Israel launched a massive aid programme with the help and support of international bodies such as the United Nations, but this had to be cut back due to Arab pressure on the recipients. It is now expanding again, and even countries which do not have diplomatic relations with Israel, such as Sri Lanka and Uganda, send students to learn about Israeli farming methods. Over the years, Israel has trained more than 27,000 overseas students, and sent 9,000 experts abroad to train local people on the spot and initiate cooperative farming projects in the third world.

One cannot write about Israel's industrial production without mentioning the arms industry, of which the Uzi submachine gun is probably the most famous product. Tanks, guns, rockets and

fighter planes have all been exported to help fund Israel's massive defence spending.

The tourist industry benefits all parts of the country, urban and rural, Jew and Arab. Over a million tourists visit Israel every year, spending $1-billion. The Ministry of Tourism has a target of two million visitors. There is every type of tourist accommodation in Israel, from the well-appointed and very economical chain of 32 youth hostels (the largest chain for a country of its size in the International Youth Hostels Association) to five-star luxury hotels. In fact, Israel positively encourages back-packing youngsters as well as the luxury trade and this adds greatly to its charm for tourists. Not only are there hotels in the big towns and seaside resorts, but there are 30 kibbutz guest-houses, as luxurious as any good hotel, where one can relax in beautiful rural surroundings. There are also Christian hospices run by the clergy in Jerusalem, Haifa, Nazareth, Tiberias and other parts of Galilee, and more than a dozen camping sites.

The Israeli workforce is very largely unionized. Some 1.5 million workers, both Jewish and non-Jewish, belong to the Histadrut, the Israel Federation of Labour. Israel has always granted equal pay to the 37 per cent of working women, and has a tradition of equality in occupations, though one no longer sees women building roads as the Jewish pioneer women did in the 1920s and 1930s before the establishment of the state. A higher proportion of Arab women, 10 per cent, go out to work than in any Arab country, compared with none at all in 1948. The lifestyle of the Israeli Arab woman is far more liberated than that of her counterpart in the Arab countries, though she still does not have the independence from family pressures enjoyed by Jewish women in Israel.

Workers' welfare is looked after by the national insurance scheme; the Histadrut sick fund, to which all members belong, looks after their health. The biggest problem faced by Israeli workers is the galloping inflation which has hit so many Third World countries, made worse in Israel's case by the gigantic but enforced defence spending. More of Israel's gross national product goes into defence than any other country's. Inflation has been brought more or less under control and faith restored in the new shekel, Israel's latest unit of currency.

Wages are lower than in western Europe or the United States, and one has to work hard for a living, but there are many privileges and plenty of job security for the wage-earner. All this encourages workers to express the initiative and quick-thinking that has often been all that stood between Israel's existence and its extinction.

THE ISRAELI ECONOMY

INDUSTRIAL PRODUCTION IN 1982

	Total Production	Export
Metals and machinery Transportation equipment	36%	29%
Non-metallic minerals, print, wood, paper, rubber, plastic and other materials	8	17
Electrical and electronics	12	13
Food, beverages, tobacco	10	14
Textiles, clothing, leather	12	13
Chemicals	17	10
Mining and quarrying	5	4

GROSS NATIONAL PRODUCT 1950–1983

	GNP at constant prices U.S.$ billion	GNP per capita at constant prices in U.S.$
1950	2.2	1,710
1960	6.0	2,850
1970	13.6	4,580
1980	22.6	5,570
1983	23.8	5,824
Annual compound real growth rate	7.5%	3.8%

(Source: Israel Central Bureau of Statistics)

ARTS AND CRAFTS

LEFT *This art gallery is housed in a medieval building in the historic city of Safed in Lower Galilee. Modern sculpture is popular in Israel, especially as the biblical prohibition on graven images is interpreted to mean that no exact representations should be made of human or animal forms.*

———

. . . and he was filled with wisdom, and
understanding, and cunning to work all works in brass.'

I KINGS 7:14

———

THE ARTS HAVE a central role to play in Israel, as an expression of feeling, a continuation of traditions begun long ago in the Diaspora (or even before that in the Land of Israel itself), as an adornment and embellishment of the country, and last but not least, as an important export and tourist attraction.

The oldest of the Israeli arts are the fine arts. Israel's first art school, the Bezalel School in Jerusalem, celebrated its 100th anniversary in 1987. It was founded by Boris (Bezalel) Schatz, a court painter from Bulgaria who conceived of a Palestinian-Jewish art which would fuse the eastern and western traditions. The Bezalel Art Museum, founded in 1906, is now part of the Museum of Israel. Israeli painters have tended away from the purely abstract and towards a more expressionist form of art. This has been attributed to the very different and profound experiences of the Israeli artist when compared to the European or American modern artist.

The horrors of the Holocaust, the War of Independence and other sufferings require very different expression from the banalities of modern western life. The most notable exception to this rule is the Israeli abstractionist painter and sculptor, Ya'akov Agam, who now lives in Paris where he has become a leading artist. His work hangs in the Elysée Palace and in leading museums of art. Other well-known Israeli artists are Mordecai Ardon, winner of the Rome Prize, who has works in the Tate Gallery in London, Reuven Rubin, Jakob Steinhardt (best known for his woodcuts), Mordecai Levanon with his dreamy landscapes, Moshe Tamir, an eminent painter who is now in charge of art education all over Israel at the Ministry of Education and Culture, and Yehuda Bacon, who is best known for his depiction of Holocaust themes. Many of the haunting Jerusalem landscapes of Anna Ticho are preserved in the Ticho House, the old Turkish house in which she lived in Jerusalem.

In addition to the major art museums such as the Helena Rubinstein Pavilion of the Tel-Aviv Museum and the Israel Museum, there are many private art galleries all over the country. Many painters live on kibbutzim and Kibbutz Ein Harod has an important art museum. There are artists' colonies in Ein Hod and Safed; more recently one has been established in old Jaffa.

RIGHT *Children learning and practising drawing in the Youth Wing of the Tel-Aviv Museum. Even seven- and eight-year-olds are not considered too young to consider such abstract concepts as 'shape' and 'image', and to learn art appreciation. All the major art museums in Israel have youth wings, and art education is considered an important element in the school curriculum at all levels and in all branches of Israeli education, even for the Arabs and the ultra-orthodox Jewish communities.*

BELOW RIGHT *Fire and Water, a sculpture by the Israeli artist, Yaakov Agam (b 1928), a leading exponent of kinetic art whose work is particularly well-known in France, where he now lives. This sculpture now stands in the centre of the famous Dizengoff Square in Tel-Aviv, replacing the fountain that once stood there.*

OPPOSITE ABOVE LEFT *The art gallery in Safed, Galilee, a holy city for Jews. Safed is today a popular place for artists to live, and an artists' colony has been established there. Safed was once the home of eminent Talmudic scholars and is the site of some beautiful 15th-century synagogues.*

OPPOSITE BELOW LEFT *Stained glass by Mordecai Ardon (b 1896), who was once director of the Bezalel School of Art. Ardon is a leading Israeli artist, whose paintings hang in the world's leading modern art museums, including the Tate Gallery and the Museum of Modern Art in New York. This work is in the National Library of the Hebrew University.*

OPPOSITE RIGHT *Demonstration of glass-blowing at the Eretz-Israel Museum, which has one of the finest collections of antique and modern glass in the world. The technique of glassmaking was invented by the Phoenicians, a northern Semitic people, many of whom converted to Judaism.*

The Israeli Ministry of Education and Culture considers that art education is a national priority. Children receive training in art from the earliest age, in the religious and non-religious school networks, and in the Arab, Christian and Druze schools. The art museums resound to the cries of children of all ages taken by their teachers to look at paintings and sculptures. Israelis consider a visit to the museum to be a family occasion. The Tel-Aviv Museum and the Israel Museum both have a youth wing where young people can paint, draw and sculpt to their hearts' content, and receive teaching as well.

Israel's two major academies of fine art are the Avni School in Tel-Aviv and the Bezalel School in Jerusalem. The modern Bezalel art school teaches graphic arts, computer-assisted art, and has pottery, photography and printing sections. It has always had a crafts section whose standards are world-renowned.

Traditional skills are being replaced by new ones, especially in architecture, not a field in which Jews of the Diaspora have been particularly prominent, but one in which Israelis are making their name. The synagogue of the Hebrew University in Jerusalem, built in the 1960s, is an example of a modern prestressed concrete structure which is used as an illustration of the best of its kind in the world's leading schools of architecture. The Israeli-born architect, Moshe Safdie, established a worldwide reputation with his revolutionary apartment building at the 1967 Montreal Expo in Canada. He is now designing a whole new quarter for Jerusalem to replace the rundown central area just outside the walls near the Jaffa Gate, which was once a no-man's-land between the Israeli and Jordanian parts of the city.

JEWISH RITUAL ART

Crafts have always had enormous importance in Jewish life. The Bible contains detailed descriptions of the intricate and magnificent Temple ornaments; from that time onwards, Jewish craftsmen have striven to adorn places of worship as best they can. Something of what could be salvaged from the ruins of Europe has been brought to Israel. There are fine collections of Jewish ritual art in the Israel Museum and the Museum of the Chief Rabbinate at Hechal Shlomo in Jerusalem. In many countries, Jews were the only skilled artisans, from tinsmiths and coppersmiths (especially in Egypt) to jewellers and plastercarvers (the Yemen), and carpetmakers (Kurdistan and Bokhara). Every effort has been made to preserve and perpetuate these skills, though unfortunately some are lost forever.

RIGHT *A marriage contract (Ketuba) from Padua, Italy (1732). The landscape picture at the top depicts Jerusalem, with the Temple in the centre.*

BELOW *Gold- and silver-filigree Torah finials (rimonim), used to cover the handles of the Scrolls of the Law when the scrolls are stored in the Ark in the synagogue. These are 18th-century Polish examples.*

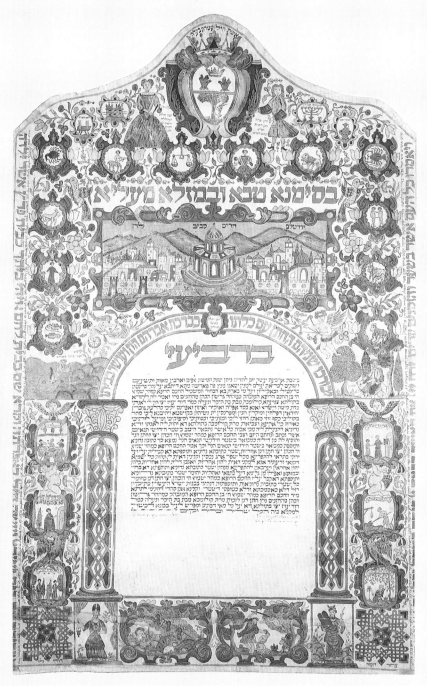

LEFT *Sabbath candlesticks in silver-anodized titanium, designed by Arie Ophir (b 1939).*

BELOW *The nine-branched Chanukah candelabra (menorah or hannukia), is given a new, ultra-modern shape by Uri Reshf (b 1955). Its material, however – brass – is very traditional.*

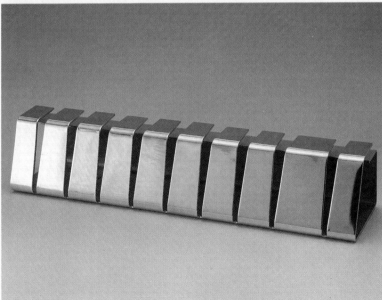

LEFT *19th-century Persian Torah scroll cases. The Oriental Jewish communities always encased the Torah in a solid case of wood or silver. In Europe, the scrolls were covered with a velvet cloth, hung from a solid cover which had two holes for the wooden handles.*

• CONTEMPORARY ART IN ISRAEL •

TOP Windows, 1972, an oil on
canvas, is by the French-born Israeli
artist Liliane Klapisch.

ABOVE Circles, by Menashe
Kadishman (b 1932), stands in the
Hebrew University campus on Mount
Scopus, Jerusalem. It is made of steel and
was produced in 1977.

ABOVE Marcel Janco (1895–1984) was
a leading Israeli artist of Romanian
origin who also worked in Paris.
Pictured is Wounded Soldier in the
Night, an oil on cardboard.

ABOVE Avigdor Arikha (b 1929), an artist of world stature, is also of Romanian extraction. Going Out is an oil on canvas, painted in 1981.

TOP Anna Ticho (1894-1980) was a famous landscapist. Her lovely old home in Jerusalem is now a museum housing many of her works. This view of the Jerusalem hills is a charcoal drawing on paper.

ABOVE One of the younger generation of artists, Pinchas Cohen Gan (b 1942) produces abstract works, many of them three-dimensional. The Other Science in Grey is a triptych in acrylic on cardboard with wooden collage.

BAT-DOR DANCE COMPANY

THE DANCE

Yemenite influence is also evident in the field of dance. Dancing has been a traditional way for Jews to let off steam, and it is still a major feature of weddings, especially ultra-orthodox (Hassidic) weddings. Israel's national dance is the hora, performed in a ring with steps so simple that anyone can learn it. Israeli folk dancing was, and still is, a popular pastime in rural settlements and many young Zionists learn the steps in youth movements abroad.

Israeli professional dance is generally modernistic, in the Martha Graham tradition, though the immigration of the Soviet classical ballet dancers, Irina and Valery Panov, who teach at the ballet school of the Rubin Academy of Music and Dance in Jerusalem, has had a profound influence, and there is now a professional troupe, the Israeli Ballet. There are a number of modern dance troupes: Inbal, consisting mainly of Yemenite dancers, the Jerusalem Dance Company, Bat-Sheva and Bat-Dor. Most of these have their own training schools.

Kol U'Demama (Sound and Silence) is a dance company unique in the world; its members consist of dancers who are deaf as well as those who can hear. The dancers who can hear give visual signs to the deaf dancers, which are incorporated into the choreography. The deaf dancers can feel the rhythm of the music through the vibrations in the floor.

THE THEATRE

Something has been said about Israeli playwrights in the chapter entitled 'The People of the Book'. Israel has an important and thriving theatre, both in Hebrew and in Arabic, although neither Jewish nor Arabic culture has ever been strong in this field (no doubt as part of the prohibition shared by both Judaism and Islam against graven images or human representations of the divine). Through centuries in the Diaspora, Jews have come to prominence in all branches of the theatre worldwide, and have produced famous actors and especially actresses, such as Eleonora Duse and Sarah Bernhardt.

In 1948, the year when the State of Israel was established, Hebrew theatre was just 30 years old. The oldest company in Israel, the country's equivalent of a national theatre, is the Ha-Bimah (The Stage) Company, founded in Moscow in 1918, under the auspices of the eminent director, Konstantin Stanislavsky; it finally made its home in Israel in 1932. Its most famous play is An-ski's *The Dybbuk* (a type of ghost which takes over a human

OPPOSITE The Bat-Dor dance company is one of several Israeli modern dance companies. Here they are performing their tribute to Edith Piaf, the French singer, entitled Piaf Vandeville. The ballerina in the centre is the company's leading dancer, Jeanette Ordman.

body). Ha-Bimah's leading lady is the actress, Hanna Meiron, a child star in pre-war Germany.

The Ohel (Tent) Company was formed by the Histadrut (the Israel Federation of Labour); in its early years it tended to perform European plays in translation. Unfortunately, the Ohel troupe could not survive financially and broke up in 1969.

The Cameri (Chamber) Theatre, formed in 1944, strove for a truly Israeli-Jewish drama, which it achieved spectacularly with its first play, *Hoo Halakh Be-Sadot (He Walked Through the Fields)* by Moshe Shamir. This tale of kibbutz life was a true expression of socialist realism. Gone were the high-flown exaggerations of classical drama; the characters behaved and talked like real people, using everyday slang.

Today, Israel has a wide variety of imported and home-grown plays and musicals for public viewing. The main theatre centre is Tel-Aviv, though Haifa has an active theatre life, with Jerusalem running behind.

Internationally known plays translated into Hebrew and performed in recent years include Tennessee Williams's *A Streetcar Named Desire*, Peter Weiss' *Marat-Sade* (performed by the Haifa Municipal Theatre), and Bertolt Brecht's *The Caucasian Chalk Circle*, and American musicals such as *My Fair Lady* and, inevitably, *Fiddler on the Roof*. Homegrown Israeli musicals have also been very popular. Perhaps the two best were *Tel-Aviv Ha-Ketana (Little Tel-Aviv)* about life in Tel-Aviv in its early years, and *Kazablán*, starring the Moroccan-born pop star, Yehoram Gaon, the story of a Moroccan immigrant in Israel. There is also a youth theatre and the Hebrew University, Tel-Aviv University and Haifa University have schools of drama. The Little English Theatre in Jerusalem is an amateur group made up of native English speakers, which has an interesting repertory. Among their most successful productions have been *The Bald Soprano* by Eugene Ionesco and *Krapp's Last Tape* by Samuel Beckett.

Today, the Israeli stage and cinema have abandoned a romanticized past and concentrate on an embittered present. They have grown up, producing sophisticated dramas which give rise to thought. Among the recent films which have won acclaim is *Ha-Ayit (The Vulture)*, 1986, about the guilt felt by a survivor of the Yom Kippur War, who is given the task of erecting monuments

MUSIC

The art at which Jews have traditionally excelled throughout the world is that of music. Music has a vital role in Israeli life, and the country's musical life is among the richest in the world.

The music industry started to take shape before the establishment of the state, in the period between the two world wars, as a result of the mass immigration of European Jews. The newcomers were particularly fond of classical music, and their numbers included many professional musicians, composers and music teachers. No longer did the Jewish community have to rely on the services of imported musicians, who did not like to come to the musical backwater of Palestine anyway – although they found enthusiastic and knowledgeable audiences when they did come.

The Palestine (later Israel) Symphony Orchestra was founded in 1936, the same year the Palestine Broadcasting Authority was inaugurated. Hed Arzi, the first recording company, was founded 10 years later.

The Palestine Symphony had two distinguished founders of international reputation: the cellist, Bronislaw Huberman, and the conductor, Arturo Toscanini (a non-Jew powerfully opposed to the rise of Fascism). After independence, the orchestra's name was changed to the Israel Philharmonic Orchestra.

In the beginning the Palestine Symphony Orchestra was just a chamber ensemble, but it later grew to a full-sized symphony orchestra.

For many years the Jerusalem Symphony Orchestra of the Israel Broadcasting Authority has been giving weekly concerts around the country. In the 1960s some of the string players in the orchestra set up a chamber orchestra.

Many great international artists have been brought in to complement the growing number of native Israeli musicians. Such artistes themselves view it as a great honour to have performed with such prestigious ensembles as the Israel Philharmonic Orchestra. They include the Indian-born conductor, Zubin Mehta, who has been associated with the IPO for over 20 years, and American musicians such as Yehudi Menuhin, Isaac Stern and Leonard Bernstein, who make frequent visits to Israel to perform.

It was once feared that as the European-born Jews gradually died out and Jews born outside the European classical tradition became the majority, the great Israeli orchestras would lose support and the importance of classical music would dwindle and disappear.

In fact, the reverse has happened. It is now, just as it always was, difficult to obtain tickets to performances of the IPO, the Haifa Symphony Orchestra, the Israel Sinfonietta (founded in Beer-Sheba) or the Netanya Orchestra. Chamber music groups are sprouting up all over the country. There is hardly any major city, town, moshav or kibbutz which does not have one – and their performances are always sold out.

LEFT *Doron Tabori and Ilan Toran of the Haifa Municipal Theatre in* Ghetto, *a play by the Israeli playwright, Yehoshua Sobol, about the Holocaust.*

BELOW *A scene from* The Avenue (Ha-Shderah), *a modern Israeli play by Ira Dabir, performed by the Habima Theatre Company. Old people are demonstrating against the uprooting of trees on their favourite avenue. The leading actors are Shmuel Rodensky and Yaakov Shabtai.*

THE CINEMA

The theatre has provided many performers for Israeli television and film. The Israeli film industry became firmly established only in the 1960s, with the formation of Capital Films and the now multinational conglomerate, Cannon. Early successes were mainly comedies such as the wildly funny *Salah Shabbati* (about a Jewish immigrant from an anonymous Arab country, which poked fun at Israeli life in general) and *The Blaumilch Canal* (about a mythical scheme to flood Dizengoff Road, Tel-Aviv's most fashionable street, to turn Tel-Aviv into the Venice of the Middle East). Musical comedies such as *Tevye and His Daughters*, a much more faithful rendering of the original Sholem Aleichem stories used in *Fiddler on the Roof*, and *Shnai Kuni Lemel*, based on a Yiddish story, were equally popular.

LEFT *Scene from the first major Israeli film, Salah Shabbati, a comedy about an immigrant from an unspecified Middle Eastern or North African country. It starred Topol, who was later to become known internationally.*

BELOW *Tevye and His Daughters was an Israeli version of the short story by Sholem Aleichem on which the smash hit, Fiddler on the Roof, was based. Many of the exterior scenes were shot in Yugoslavia, since there is no Israeli landscape that resembles Poland closely enough.*

Whenever a foreign orchestra comes to visit, it is almost impossible to get a ticket. Fortunately, Tel-Aviv Municipality and the IPO hold an open-air, free concert once a year at the beginning of the summer. Usually over 50,000 people come and listen to the concert, which always has a spectacular finale: Tchaikovsky's 1812 Overture, with a marvellous fireworks display substituting for the cannons called for by the score.

Israeli musicians such as the violinist Itzhak Perlman, the pianist and conductor, Daniel Barenboim, the pianists, Shlomo Mintz and Gideon Rosengarten, and one of the world's few women conductors, Dalia Atlas, have achieved international renown.

Opera too is regaining popularity in Israel. Several years ago, the Opera House in Tel-Aviv was closed and the company disbanded. However, there has been a lot of public demand for opera and foreign companies have successfully toured the country. Featured luminaries have included the tenor Placido Domingo, who coincidentally started his professional career in Israel and had his first long-term singing contract with the Tel-Aviv Opera House, and the superstar tenor, Luciano Pavarotti.

There is even a group that performs nothing but the operettas of Gilbert and Sullivan – the Logan Group, made up of English-speaking academics from the Ben-Gurion University of the Negev in Beer-Sheba.

The annual Zimria Choir Festival also attracts a lot of local and international talent. Many kibbutzim and moshavim have their own choirs, dating back to the days when the Jewish pioneers had to make their own entertainment in the remote settlements.

Music teaching is considered to be extremely important, and begins from an early age. Music academies were founded in Palestine as early as 1910, 1914 and 1918. They have now evolved into the Rubin Academy of Tel-Aviv and Jerusalem. In addition, there are departments of musicology at Tel-Aviv University, Bar-Ilan University and the Hebrew University. Today more Israelis than ever are interested in studying the western classical tradition. Both the Rubin Academy of Music in Jerusalem and the Thelma Yellin School of the Performing Arts, in Givatayim near Tel-Aviv, are always oversubscribed. Both conform to the highest standards.

However, lest we believe that all Israelis are high-brow and go around toting violins, it would be a good idea at this point to mention contemporary music.

For the first 25 years of Israel's existence, a lot of the pop music was based on the old eastern European ballads. Western pop music was, to say the least, looked down upon as being somehow 'unpatriotic'. Jewish music in the Arab tradition fared even worse. It was not even played on the radio, with the exception of songs sung by Shoshana Damari – perhaps because her Yemenite-inspired music was carefully arranged by a European composer, Moshe Smilansky. Successive young Israeli musicans have tried to bring a more contemporary western sound to their music.

In the country's formative years in the 1950s and 1960s, the army troupes, which travelled around the country entertaining the soldiers at the front and pioneer settlers, enjoyed great popularity. Many of the country's more popular artistes started their careers with these troupes. Chava Alberstein and Arik Ainshtain began this way and went on to become two of the country's top recording stars. Their music is very nostalgic, and contains a yearning for the days of innocence before independence. Both have also recorded traditional songs in Yiddish.

Jewish folk music is as old as Judaism itself, and, thanks to the efforts of Emil Berliner, the Jewish music publisher who invented the flat photograph record in 1897, it was one of the first types of music to be put on disk. In Israel, Jewish folk music is researched and recorded as a priority.

Today there are three different strands in Israeli contemporary music. First, there is what is known as Oriental music, the Jewish musical style from the Arab countries, which westernized Jews may not like but which has a large following.

At first, Israeli record companies would not sign Oriental artistes. This led the singers and the songwriters to start recording on their own; thus developed the 'Cassette Singers' (*Zamarei Kassetot*) industry. Around the Tel-Aviv central bus station, there are dozens of shops selling 'bootleg' recordings of these singers. Lately, more radio air-time has been given to the musicians. Their music talks about love, social problems and life in general. The melodies are based on the music of their countries of origin – the Yemen, Morocco, Libya, Iran and Iraq. One singer of this type of music, Ofra Haza, a Yemenite who grew up in a Tel-Aviv slum, gained international recognition when her song 'Galbi' became a very popular disco song in England. As a result, her record of Yemenite songs has sold more than 10,000 copies in Britain and has become something of a cult favourite.

The second strand of popular Israeli music is the modern type, which started at the end of the 1970s when many Israeli youths travelled abroad. They saw the punk revolution in Europe and wanted a similar one at home. Groups like Syam, Chromosome, and The Intensive Care Unit started performing in the clubs of Tel-Aviv. These clubs, with their dark, oppressive decor, started cropping up in the city like toadstools after a rain. They had names like Underground, which had maps of the London tube system on the walls, Penguin and Liquid. Young people began

LEFT *Studying the harp at the Rubin Academy of Music in Jerusalem. Israel hosts an international harp festival, held once every four years, which is an important event in the international musical calendar.*

walking around with coloured hair and safety pins through their noses – the government almost thought it had a new Jewish Revolt on its hands.

Recently, though, a third strand of music – more relaxed – has become prevalent on the Israeli charts. The music *does* talk about the problems confronting the modern Israeli, but it is sung in much more dulcet tones.

The new trend is represented by singers like Shalom Hanoch, whose song 'Messiah Does Not Come – He Does Not Even Give Us a Ring' became an instant hit when it spoke of the economic and political problems which face the country. A singing duo of this type, Rita and Yehudit Ravitz, are constantly 'top of the pops'.

Israeli contemporary music follows the fashion of its English-language counterparts more closely nowadays, although there is still a following for songs about the good old days of Eretz Yisrael, including Zionist pioneer songs such as 'Night Has Fallen' ('Rad Ha-daila') and 'The Valley is a Dream' ('Ha-Emek Hoo Halom'). Songs based on passages from the Bible, such as 'And You Shall Draw Water with Joy from the Well of Salvation' ('Ushavtem Mayim') and 'My Beloved Is Mine and I Am His ('Dodi Li') from the Song of Solomon, are also popular.

All these types of music, plus the music from neighbouring Arab radio stations, Israel's own Arab Broadcasting Network, and the standard 'middle-of-the-road' American music played on Israel's Light Wave Network, make for an enormous range of music catering to every taste.

THE JEWISH CALENDAR

The Jewish calendar is based on the ancient Canaanite calendar, and is fundamentally lunar. The hour is divided into 1,080 parts or *minim*; each month is reckoned at 29 days, 12 hours and 793 *minim*. The present calendar was fixed by the Patriarch Hillel II, under Roman rule, in AD 358, and the months are adjusted to the solar year, so that the festivals fall at almost exactly the same season each year. There is a 19-year cycle, in which there are seven years containing an extra or leap month. These years, the third, sixth, eighth, eleventh, fourteenth, seventeenth and nineteenth are known as *shana meuberet*. The extra 30-day month is inserted before the month of Adar and is known as Adar Sheni. In a leap year the month of Adar itself has 30 days instead of 29. The Jewish day formally commences six hours before midnight, which in practice means that all Jewish festivals begin at dusk on the festival eve. In fact, the same practice used to be adopted by Christianity, hence the importance of Christmas Eve.

The months of the Jewish calendar and their roughly corresponding months in the Christian calendar are as follows:

Nissan	March/April
	25th Nissan: Passover (Pesach)
Iyyar	April/May
	18th Iyyar: Lag Be-Omer
Sivan	May/June
	6th Sivvan: Shavuot (Feast of Weeks, Pentecost or Festival of the First Fruits)
Tammuz	June/July
Av	July/August
	9th of Av: Fast of Av (Tisha B'Av)
Elul	August/September
Tishri	September-October
	1st Tishri: Rosh Ha-Shana (New Year)
	10th Tishri: Yom Kippur (Day of Atonement)
	15th Tishri: Sukkot (Feast of Tabernacles)
	22nd Tishri: Simhat Torah (Rejoicing of the Law)
Heshvan	October-November
Kislev	November/December
	25th Kislev: Chanukah (Festival of Lights)
Tevet	December/January
Shevat	January/February
	15th Shevat: New Year for Trees (Tu Bishevat)
(Adar Sheni)	Periodic leap month
Adar	February/March
	14th Adar: Purim (Feast of Lots or Feast of Esther)

ISRAEL
AT PLAY

LEFT *Enjoying the hot springs at Hamat Gader in the Jordan Valley. The nearby remains of an ancient synagogue with a beautiful mosaic floor are an added bonus for a pleasant outing.*

148

'Let Mount Zion rejoice, let the daughters of Judah
be glad . . .'

PSALM 48:11

LEISURE IS A PRECIOUS COMMODITY in
Israel, since the Israelis get so little of it. The
Jewish Sabbath is the only official rest day of the
week in all but Christian and Moslem communities, which each observe their own sabbaths.
Government offices, though, wherever they are located, are always closed on Saturday, the Jewish Sabbath.

All Jewish religious holidays last from sunset to sunset. This
effectively turns Friday into a half-day, or more accurately, a three-
quarter day in summer and a half-day in winter. Civil servants stop
work on Friday at 1:30 PM in winter, 3:30 PM in summer (they start
at 8:00 AM), and do not work Saturdays. Sunday is the first day of
the working week, the day of the weekly meeting of the Israeli
cabinet.

Saturday is a very quiet day in Israel. No public places of entertainment are open (at least officially), there are no buses except in
Haifa (and Arab buses in Arab areas of the country) and no trains,
though if you want to travel you can get a *sherut* (shared taxi)
between the big cities, or use a private car.

Orthodox Jews are forbidden by their religion to light fires on
the Sabbath. They solve the problem by using automatic lights on
timers or keeping certain electrical installations on from sunset to
sunset on the Sabbath. In kosher hotels, meals are prepared before
the Sabbath and are either served cold or kept warm on hotplates.
The lifts (elevators) are set to automatic so that on the Sabbath the
doors open on each floor and no buttons need be pushed. Smok-
ing in the public areas of kosher hotels is forbidden on the Sabbath.

The streets of Jewish cities are deserted on Saturdays – until
after dusk. That is the time for the mass promenade, especially of
young people, the only true leisure time in the week. Tel-Aviv
and Jerusalem turn into miniature carnivals every Saturday night;
cafés and kiosks selling soft drinks, felafel (Israel's national dish,
ground chickpeas fried in oil) and kebabs in pita bread do a roaring
trade.

The major Jewish festivals are also public holidays. Although
the Jewish calendar begins in the spring, the Jewish New Year
celebration falls in the autumn, which is logical because this is the
start of the agricultural year in the Middle East, the time of the

RIGHT *Inside the Caro synagogue in
Safed. This synagogue is dedicated to the
memory of Joseph Caro, a Safed scholar
who compiled a sacred work called the
Shulhan Arukh, a codification of all
the laws in the Talmud.*

BELOW *Blowing the ram's horn
(shofar) on the Jewish New Year at the
Western Wall. It is customary at New
Year and the Day of Atonement to cover
the head with the prayer shawl (tallit)
as a sign of repentance.*

OPPOSITE *In Jerusalem it is now
customary for Jews to go to the Western
Wall (once called the Wailing Wall)
to pray on the Sabbath.*

THE SABBATH AT THE WESTERN WALL

first rains. The Jewish calendar, which is also the ancient Canaanite calendar, is moon-based. The twelve months are alternatively 29 and 30 days long. An extra short month of 11 days is inserted seven times within every 19 years in the spring to bring it in line with the sun calendar, thus ensuring that festivals fall at approximately the same season every year. The Jewish calendar is supposed to date from the day on which the rabbis calculated the earth was created, which was 3761 BC. The Jews are thus in the 7th century of the 6th millennium (1989 is 5749 in the Jewish calendar).

In addition to the religious festivals, two days are commemorated in Israel which are not part of the Jewish religious calendar. The first is Holocaust Remembrance Day, which occurs on the 27th day of Nissan, and is a half-holiday. Two minutes' silence is observed throughout the country for the Jews who have died in

RIGHT *A young Israeli plants a tree at Kibbutz Ein Ha-Horesh on Tu Bishevat, the New Year of the Trees. Even in kibbutzim which are not religious and where there are no synagogue services, the Jewish festivals are celebrated with enthusiasm.*

persecutions of Jews throughout the ages. The other day, which is a full public holiday, is Israel Independence Day, which falls on the 5th day of Iyyar (April or May).

Israelis working in the public sector take time off on the major holidays. The last day of several seven-day festivals is also a public holiday, except in the case of Chanukah, the Festival of Lights. The minor holidays are the New Year of the Trees, Purim, Lag Be-Omer (midway between Passover and Shavuot, 1st of May (when there are workers' parades in Tel-Aviv and Haifa), 9th of Av (a fast day on which by tradition both the first and second Temples were destroyed) and the first day of Chanukah.

Although in the Diaspora, the New Year and several other Jewish festivals are celebrated for two days, in Israel only one day is observed. This is because outside Israel people could not be sure whether they were actually celebrating on the right day.

The New Year, or Rosh Ha-Shana, marks the start of a group of festivals known collectively as the High Holidays. It is followed by the most solemn day in the Jewish year, Yom Kippur – the Day of Atonement. This is a total fast day, on which no food or drink may be taken from sunset to sunset. In the towns and cities nothing moves. Everyone is at home or in synagogue – the perfect day for an enemy to start a war, which happened, of course, in 1973.

Immediately the Day of Atonement is over, there is a complete change of mood, for the celebration of Sukkot – the Feast of Tabernacles. This is one of the three harvest festivals, and it also celebrates the arrival of the Israelites in the Promised Land, when they hurriedly erected temporary dwellings or booths. The festival is celebrated for its seven days by the erection of such booths outside houses or on the balconies of apartments. In fact, in religious neighbourhoods, the balconies of apartments are specially constructed so that they are not completely aligned on top of each other, since the booth must have a roof through which the sky can be seen.

The Festival of Sukkot lasts eight days in Israel (outside of Israel most major festivals last a day longer because of differences in the perception of the new moon). On the eighth day, a special day is celebrated called Shemini Atzeret (The Eighth Day of Solemn Assembly), because in Numbers 29:35, it states 'On the eighth day ye shall have a solemn assembly: ye shall do no servile work therein'. In Israel, this falls on the same day as Simhat Torah, the Rejoicing of the Law, an exuberant celebration, particularly among the ultra-orthodox. In Jewish practice, a set portion is read in synagogue on the Sabbath from the Torah, the Five Books of Moses, in an annual cycle. The Rejoicing of the Law celebrates the end of

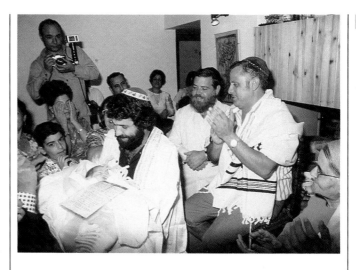

LEFT *The dedication of a new* Sefer Torah *(Scroll of the Law), at the Western Wall. The men wear* tefillin *on their foreheads and wrists, little boxes bound with leather thongs which contain passages from the Scriptures. It must be a weekday, since the tefillin are not worn on the Sabbath and festival days. The community is probably of Sephardic (Spanish) or Oriental origin, because the scroll is in a solid case; the Ashkenazic (German and Polish) communities cover their scrolls with a decorated cloth.*

RIGHT *Circumcision ceremony in a religious kibbutz. The man who holds the baby for the ceremony is the* sandak, *or godfather, who bears a special responsibility for the boy throughout his life.*

LEFT *Choosing an* etrog *(citron) is a serious business. The fruit must be absolutely perfect and free of any blemishes. It should also have a 'nipple' (*pitma*) on the end opposite the stem, which is actually the withered flower bud.*

one yearly cycle and the beginning of the next. All the scrolls are taken out of the Ark, the cupboard in the synagogue where they are normally housed, and paraded joyously round the synagogue and sometimes out in the open, at the Western Wall in Jerusalem, for instance. Members of the congregation follow the procession, waving flags, and the children receive candy.

The next festival, Chanukah, is another minor festival from the religious point of view, because it is the only Jewish festival which does not centre on a biblical event. Chanukah, the Festival of Lights, commemorates the victory of the Maccabees over the evil Seleucid conquerors of Judah. After the Seleucids had desecrated the Temple in Jerusalem it had to be reconsecrated, but only a small container of oil, enough to last one day, could be found to light the Eternal Lamp. More supplies would take a week to arrive, yet the tiny amount of oil miraculously lasted for a full eight days. For this reason, a special nine-branched candlestick, or *menorah* (originally containing oil lamps), is lit during the festival, for the eight days, plus the *shamash*; an extra light which is used to light the others. The festival starts with just one light plus the *shamash* and an extra one is added every day, until all nine are lit. The story appears in the Book of the Maccabees in the Apocrypha, a collection of post-biblical writings.

Chanukah is a very jolly but minor festival. It is not an official holiday, so there are none of the restrictions on travelling or making fire which apply to the major festivals. Since it is a commandment for the Chanukah lights to be displayed, public buildings are illuminated with huge Chanukah lamps, and people place them in the windows of their homes so they can be seen from the street.

THE FESTIVAL OF THE FIRST FRUITS

After Chanukah, in early spring (still winter in the United States and Europe) there is Hag-Ha-Ilanot, the New Year for Trees, commonly known as Tu Bishevat, or the 15th day of Shevat, the date on which the festival occurs. This is the day for tree-planting and is especially important to schoolchildren of all ages.

The biggest of the fun festivals, Purim – the Feast of Lots – occurs in March. This is the commemoration of the story of Esther, the Jewish queen married to a Persian king who, with her cousin Mordecai, saved her people from destruction by the wicked Haman, the king's minister, who has come to symbolize the archetype of an anti-semite. It is carnival time; in the Diaspora, Purim plays were traditional and actors went from house to house performing in Jewish villages. In Israel, the carnival takes place outdoors. There are big parades in Jerusalem and Tel-Aviv and children and young people throng the streets wearing fancy dress. This can lead to some amusing confrontations. Genuine Arabs tend to encounter fake 'Arabs' in elaborate headdresses and robes, and real Hassidic Jews meet their fancy-dress counterparts adorned with false beards and fake sidelocks.

A quaint Purim custom is that of Mishloah Manot – the Sending of Portions – when people pack up a small parcel of goodies, cakes and candies, and send them to neighbours. The synagogue service is a raucous affair, because the children bring rattles and other noisemakers with them, which they sound off every time the name of the wicked Haman is mentioned in the reading from the Scroll of Esther.

A month later there is another very solemn festival, one whose meaning is all too relevant today – Pesah, the Festival of Passover. Jews all over the world hold the traditional banquet, or *seder*, to commemorate the Exodus of the Jews from Egypt. A place is laid and a cup prepared for the prophet Elijah, the absent guest. Some people lay another place for another absent guest – the Jew detained against his will in a country from which he cannot escape, such as the USSR, Syria or Iraq.

The Passover order of service is contained in a special prayerbook, the Haggadah, which is usually lavishly illustrated. Magnificent examples of illuminated medieval Haggadot exist in museums; there is one, donated by the Rothschild family, in the Israel Museum.

Exactly 50 days later the last major festival of the Jewish year is celebrated, one which like Tabernacles and Passover lasts seven days because it used to be a festival of pilgrimage to Jerusalem. It is Shavuot, the Feast of Weeks, so called because it falls seven weeks after Passover. It is also known as Hag Habikkurim, the Festival of First Fruits, when the early harvest – which today consists mainly

of peaches, apricots, cherries and the first grain harvest – is gathered in. It also commemorates the giving of the Torah (the Law) to Moses on Mount Sinai.

Like all the other festivals, the Feast of Weeks is associated with a particular food. In this case it is dairy foods, such as blintzes (crêpes), filled with cottage cheese and cream cheese, and ruby-red borscht (beet soup), topped with a generous dollop of sour cream.

For Passover, the food is unique, as it must be completely free of leaven. Because the Israelites had to flee so quickly, they had no time to bake their bread properly, so it dried out on their backs without rising. Hence the eating of *matzot*, unleavened bread, for the whole week of the festival. Before the festival, the house is cleaned from top to bottom and a search is made for crumbs of leaven, which are then ceremonially burned. The sages of old did not have the benefit of modern chemical knowledge, and their idea of leaven was a bit hazy. Hence, nothing may be made with ordinary flour, though flour made from ground unleavened bread (matzot) may be eaten, as well as potato flour. Wine is permitted, though beer is forbidden. Nor did all the sages agree on what was allowed and what was forbidden; Ashkenazi Jews are forbidden to eat rice, peas or beans, but the Sephardim are allowed all of these.

Vast amounts of eggs are eaten during the Passover week. People can be seen carrying large egg boxes; it is just as well eggs

OPPOSITE *Children offering the first fruits on the Feast of Weeks (Shavuot), also known as Pentecost or the Festival of the First Fruits (Hag Ha-Bikkurim). It is traditional to eat dishes made with milk and cheese on this festival, which also celebrates the giving of the Law to Moses.*

ABOVE A *family eating the Passover meal in Tel-Aviv. The book lying on the table is the Haggadah, the special order of service for Passover, written partly in Hebrew and partly in Aramaic, a related language that was commonly spoken around the time of Jesus Christ.*

• EATING OUT •

ABOVE *Inside a Jerusalem felafel bar. The green and red foods in the bowls are hot pickled peppers and pickled turnips in beetroot (beet) juice. Standards of hygiene are the highest in the Middle East. Felafel is a deep-fried ball of spiced ground chickpeas (garbanzos) and field beans, which is the national dish of both Israel and Egypt.*

TOP *Inside an elegant restaurant in the Old City of Jerusalem. The low seating is traditional. Specialities of the house include honey-roast pigeon with pine nuts and baked lamb in tahina sauce.*

are in season! Eggs are symbolic of spring and the life cycle in Jewish custom. At Purim, three-cornered cakes called Haman's Ears (*Oznay Haman*) or Haman's pockets (*Hamantaschen*) filled with poppyseed or puréed prunes are traditional among Ashkenazic communities. Other communities eat fried pastries dipped in honey with the same or a similar name.

At the Festival of Lights it is traditional to eat foods cooked in oil, such as doughnuts and potato pancakes, and these are particularly well-suited to the mid-winter climate.

New Year and the High Holidays are the time for honey and apple and honey cakes, sweetness to symbolize a sweet New Year. The various Jewish communities of Israel have their own traditional festival foods, which have been amalgamated into a cuisine which is uniquely Israeli. Although there are some Ashkenazi-style restaurants, selling the heavy European dishes traditionally cooked in goose fat, but now prepared with chicken fat, the fact that they are so few in number compared to the population which must have been raised on them is indicative of their popularity. Far more popular are the 'Oriental' and Yemenite restaurants, serving lean meats such as kebabs (called *shashlik* in Israel; kebab is grilled ground meat) in pita, with plenty of salad dressed with *tahina* (ground sesame seed mixed with oil), a big slice of lemon and some spicy, crushed green olives.

Both the Rejoicing of the Law and the Feast of Lots are traditional times for heavy drinking, but Israelis are generally very abstemious. Perhaps it is the Middle Eastern temperament, because Arabs are not drinkers either (the Moslem religion forbids alcohol, but this would never deter the determined); there is also the fact that wine-drinking is an important part of Jewish ritual even for the young. A blessing is said over the wine every Sabbath evening, and four glasses of wine must be drunk at the *seder* meal. Israel produces a large range of fine wines and almost every other kind of alcoholic drink (except whisky), from flavoured vodkas to arak and brandy. Alcohol can be bought and consumed at any time of the day or night from licensed premises. In practice, these consist of grocery stores or speciality food stores where alcohol can be bought to take out, and bars in the big cities. Many restaurants and cafés also sell alcohol, but not all.

The favourite drink in Israel, of Arabs and Israelis alike, is coffee. Israelis drink espresso, but they and the Arabs also enjoy the rich, black Turkish-style coffee, into which cardamon seed (*hel*) is dropped (by the Jews) or ground (by the Arabs) to give it a rich aroma.

A tiny cup of this strong brew will revive you as nothing else can, even in the worst heat of the summer.

• ISRAELI FOOD •

LEFT *Strawberries are a major Israeli export. The season begins as early as March and is at its height in May. In the strawberry season, these easily perishable fruits are available at knock down prices in the street markets of Israel. These shoppers are eyeing the display on a stall in Jerusalem's Mahaneh Yehuda market.*

BELOW *Honey-rich pastries displayed on the large trays on which they were cooked outside a shop in the Old City of Jerusalem. The Arabs do not eat dessert, but have pastries and Turkish-style coffee as a snack between meals.*

LEFT *A chef at one of Israel's luxury hotels poses by the pool with a tray of typical Israeli breakfast ingredients. Inspired by the hearty kibbutz breakfasts, eaten before a long day's manual labour, the Israeli breakfast will include the standard bread, coffee and grapefruit to be found all over the western world, but with the addition of quantities of fruit, vegetables, yoghurt, and even pickled herrings and olives.*

The Moslems celebrate their sabbath, Friday, by closing their shops and businesses and attending the mosque services. The Moslem calendar is also based on the cycles of the moon but does not try to catch up with the sun, so that holy days may take place at any time of year. An important time is Ramadan, the ninth month of the Moslem year. This period commemorates the revelation of the Koran, Islam's holy book, to Mohammed. During Ramadan eating and drinking may only take place after the sun has set. Ramadan is immediately followed by Id Al-Fitr, when it is traditional to kill and eat a sheep. Another festival commemorates the *Hejira*, Mohammed's flight from Mecca to Medina. The Moslem calendar dates from this event, which took place in 622, so the Moslem equivalent of 1989 is 1409.

All the other religious communities celebrate their festivals. Christmas and Easter are important times of Christian pilgrimage from abroad, just as Passover is a favourite time for Jews to visit Israel on pilgrimage.

What do Israelis do for relaxation? Well, whenever they get the chance, they travel. They love to visit friends and relatives, especially if these friends and relatives live at the opposite ends of the country. For many Israelis who cannot afford proper holidays, this is their only vacation. Fortunately, Israel's public transportation system is extremely inexpensive and very efficient. Least expensive of all are trains, which run between Haifa and Tel-Aviv, or Jerusalem and Tel-Aviv and Jerusalem and Haifa. The inter-urban buses run regular services to destinations all over the country, and there are shared taxis between the big cities on every day of the week, including Saturdays.

However, cheapest of all is hitchhiking. This has become slightly more dangerous since 1967 and the open borders, but it is common for young people to travel in this way, and especially in remote areas, where public transportation is not so efficient. Hitchhiking is most commonly practised by soldiers, for whom there are even special shelters while they wait for what in Israel has come to be known as a *tremp* (lift). Pay is low in the army, and precious shekels need to be saved and not spent on the trips to and from home to base camp. Fortunately, in a country so small as Israel, the home comforts are never more than a day's journey away.

SPORT IN ISRAEL

Israelis have always enjoyed physical exercise, though not necessarily competitive sports. PT is taught from nursery school upwards, and at the beaches there are always groups of enthusiasts

ABOVE *Hikers in Galilee. This is the favourite Israeli pastime and the best way to get to know the countryside.*

ranging in age from three to 93 doing physical jerks.

The first Jewish sports clubs were established in 1906 in Jaffa and Jerusalem, and a national festival was held in Rehovot in 1908. However, the first nationwide sports organization, Maccabi, named for the great Jewish hero, Judah the Maccabee, was established in 1912. It is an unfortunate fact of Israeli life that this type of organization, which in any other country would be non-political, is soon adopted by a political party. This is the case with the sick funds, and it was the case with sports. Maccabi became the sports organization of the Liberal Party (now part of the right-wing Likud), just as Betar, established in 1924, was the sports wing of the revisionist Herut party, and Elizur was founded by the Mizrahi, the National Religious Party. The biggest sports organization today is HaPoel, founded in 1926 and fostered by the Mapai, the Israel Labour Party (now the Labour Alignment).

There is also an Academic Sports Association, founded in 1953, which has nine branches in the universities and other institutes of higher education.

Maccabi is not only the oldest of the sports organizations but also the most prestigious and important, with a large network and

LEFT *Israeli international footballer Avi Cohen, who has since played for Liverpool in England. Soccer is by far the most popular spectator sport in Israel, and leading players have been snapped up by European teams.*

sports facilities outside Israel. In 1932, it staged the first Maccabiah, the Jewish Olympic Games, to which Jewish athletes came from all over the world. These included several from countries which were shortly to fall under Nazi domination yet who were allowed to compete for the glory of the Reich in the 1936 Olympic Games in Berlin. The Maccabiah is held every four years, like the Olympic Games. HaPoel also holds a four-yearly international meet.

Israel sent its first team of athletes to the Olympic Games in 1952 and has participated regularly since then, with the exception of the 1980 Moscow games. The athletes consist mainly of weight-lifters, wrestlers and footballers. Tragedy struck the Israeli team at the 1972 Munich games, when 11 of its athletes were murdered by Arab terrorists.

Israeli sports and physical education instructors and coaches are trained at the Wingate Institute of Physical Education near Netanya, and at teacher training colleges.

The Israelis' favourite sport is soccer. Israeli children have their favourite football team and players and, quite surprisingly, display an amazing knowledge of world football, especially of the British teams.

This is one result of the British Mandate of Palestine. Prior to World War I, gymnastics were the rage, but British soldiers brought their sport with them, and Jewish football clubs began sprouting up all over the country.

Israel has only participated once in the football World Cup, in Mexico, 1970. The team did quite well, drawing with Sweden and Portugal, but losing to Italy, the eventual finalists.

One of the reasons behind Israel's apparently poor performance in world soccer is the fact that football's governing body (FIFA) has had great difficulty in finding Israel an appropriate region in which to play. Israel's Arab neighbours will not play Israel and the European countries do not think it proper that an Asian team play in their region. So a compromise of sorts was found – Israel has to travel all the way to Oceania to play Australia, New Zealand and Taiwan. That is quite a distance and it takes its toll on the players. Over the past few years, a steady flow of foreign and international teams have visited Israel to play matches.

Israeli players are all technically amateur, although they do receive substantial fees from their clubs, paid for mainly by sponsorships. However, top players receive top fees, even when compared to the European scale, and this can leave the clubs on the verge of bankruptcy.

There are four divisions in the Israeli Football League, and although most of the clubs' facilities would be considered primitive by European standards, and the attendances are low, there are three stadia – the national stadium in Ramat Gan, the Bloomfield Stadium in Jaffa and the Kiryat Eliezer Stadium, near Haifa, each holding over 20,000 spectators. Over the past few years an ever-increasing number of top-class Israeli players have been joining European teams and making quite a reputation for themselves. To name but a few: Mordechai Shpiegler, who played in France and for West Ham United, and Giora Shpigel and Vicky Peretz, who have also played in France.

Currently, four Israelis are really making the grade in Europe: Ronny Rosenthal and Eli Ohanna in Belgium; and David Pizanti, who has played for FC Cologne and Queens Park Rangers. But the most famous must be Avi Cohen. He has played for Liverpool and now plays for Glasgow Rangers.

Another sport which is very popular in Israel is basketball. Here local teams have had quite a few successes at the European level. Maccabi Tel-Aviv, three times European club champions, regularly compete in the final stages of the European Basketball Championship.

During the final stages of the competition, almost the whole population of Israel watches the games on television. The streets

are deserted and after every score you can hear the roars and cheers from the houses. These games usually take place on a Thursday night. If you aren't a basketball fan, this is the best time to go to the cinema, because you'll be able to get a ticket even for the most popular films.

In the final stages of the European championship, Maccabi Tel-Aviv usually has to face a team from the Soviet Union – usually CSKA Moskva (the Red Army team) or Dynamo Kiev. It is always a great occasion when the Tel-Aviv team beats the Soviet team – people often gather at the fountain in Tel-Aviv Municipality square and jump in the water – even in winter!

Maccabi Tel-Aviv is not the only basketball team in Israel to have European successes under its belt. HaPoel Tel-Aviv and Ha-Poel Galil Elyon have reached the latter stages of the European Cup Winners Cup and the Korac Cup on numerous occasions over the past few years. The Israeli national basketball team is also a source of pride, having reached the final stages of both European and world championships.

Both football and basketball, as well as track and field and

OPPOSITE TOP *Basketball champions Maccabi Tel-Aviv, who beat the whole of Europe on several occasions.*

OPPOSITE BELOW *Athlete Esther Rot competing in the hurdles. Israel has not produced women athletes of international renown, largely due to the problems of finding adequate training facilities.*

LEFT *Amos Mansdorf, who, along with Shlomo Glikstein, is one of Israel's leading tennis stars. He is seen here competing in the Lipton Tournament in Florida in 1988.*

gymnastics, are taught at the school level. All local teams have a youth wing so young aspiring players and athletes can get a chance to make it.

Another sport which caught on beginning in the 1970s in a big way is tennis. Many youngsters took to the sport and Israel has produced some fine world-class players, like Shlomo Glikstein, and more recently, Amos Mansdorf and Gilad Bloom.

The height of the Israeli tennis team's success was the participation in the quarter-finals of the Davis Cup in India in July 1987. Unfortunately, the Indian side proved too tough a team for the Israelis and they were routed 5–0. However, reaching the quarter-finals proved to be a fantastic morale-booster for the young Israeli team, considering that they beat such tennis giants as Britain and Czechoslovakia to reach that honour.

Israel also has a motor racing track. Anyone who has been to the country and tried driving there will think that this refers to the drivers on Israel's highways and country roads – such is the notoriety of the Israeli motorist!

Nevertheless, and joking aside, over the past several years Israel

has held motor racing meetings for three types of cars – up to 1000cc, up to 1300cc and up to 1600cc – in the southern resort of Ashkelon. Although the country is not yet part of the International Grand Prix circuit, there are a few racing drivers who are looking for sponsors after passing the strenuous test which Grand Prix drivers have to face.

There are facilities for all ball sports in Israel. And because Israel is a country of immigrants, a lot of 'new' games have been introduced to the area. These were mainly introduced by those who came from the 'Anglo-Saxon' countries (an Israeli term for those who hail from the English-speaking lands, mainly Britain, Australia and South Africa). They have brought with them such delights as badminton, squash, cricket, hockey and rugby. Surprisingly, a few Israelis took to these games after they learnt the intricate, confusing rules. Other important sports in Israel are weightlifting and wrestling. The main interest in these sports comes from North African, Bulgarian and Russian immigrants. Israel regularly participates in Olympic events in these sports and does quite well, in the tradition of Samson.

There is even an 18-hole golf course at Caesarea, which has recently started teaching underprivileged children from the neighbouring villages, as well as catering for the golfing requirements of some tourists and those of the Israeli president, Chaim Herzog, who is a well-known golfer.

Israelis have a love for the great outdoors in general. Every holiday and festival will find Israeli families down by the beach or in the numerous national parks or on a hike. The parks are usually filled with picnickers. Every Succot (Feast of Tabernacles) there is a sponsored mass walk between the coastal plain and Jerusalem. Hundreds of thousands of soldiers and civilians take part. It usually ends with a colourful parade through the centre of the capital. There is also an annual swim across the Sea of Galilee and marathon races around Mount Tabor in the north, and around the Sea of Galilee, which usually bring in a great number of top-class foreign contestants.

Most of the events are just a way for people to get away from it all without any element of competition. Thousands participate, from every walk of life and of any and all ages – whether they are organized or not, just to get out into the fresh air. Walking in the countryside has been described as Israel's folk happening, a way of getting to know the country better.

The most significant outdoor activity for most Israelis is lapping up the sun at the beach or at the pool. For nine months of the year the beaches are inhabited, at any time of the day or night. Whether they be those who brave the crowds on a Saturday

morning in the summer or just those, who, because of the heat, prefer to spend the night on the beach because of the cool breeze or the peaceful lapping of the waves. The peace and quiet of the sea at night is often broken by the sound of beach parties. On Saturday, Israel's only 'weekend', the beaches are crammed with people. Your only worry is that you might be hit by a small rubber black ball, which is part of Israel's beach national sport – matkot.

Matkot, which literally means 'hitting', is a variation on the beach ball games played on any Mediterranean coastal resort. It consists of two people hitting a small rubber squash ball back and forth with their bare hands or a ping-pong bat with all their might, usually from a distance of 10 to 15 yards (10–15 m). They try to keep this up for as long as possible, but inevitably someone misses and the ball gets hit at innocent bystanders. It's all in good fun, but be warned.

All of Israel's Mediterranean beaches are sandy. The only really pebbly beach is on the Sea of Galilee; at the Red Sea beach at Eilat, the sand is rather coarse.

Most of the coastal resorts have invested a lot in the facilities at the seaside, realizing the full potential of the beaches. It used to be quite dangerous to venture into the sea on some days because of the strong currents and undertow, but a series of breakwaters was built in the 1970s and it is now quite safe to go into the water, even when the sea is fairly stormy. In any case, all government-approved beaches have fully trained lifeguards on duty and it is always advisable to check to see if the beach that you want to use is approved and safe.

The in thing at Israeli beaches is a water slide. These slides, which are known as 'glitz-glatz' and are cropping up all over the place, are mainly for younger children, but adults have taken to

them too. They consist of a slide or a tube running down from a height to the water's edge or into a seawater pool. The idea is, as you have probably gathered, to shoot down the slide or tube as fast as possible and make a huge splash at the other end.

There is also a surge of interest in surfing and windsurfing. Relatively unknown in Israel a few years ago, these sports have grown considerably, and almost every morning one can find a group of surfers near the beach close to the Tel-Aviv Hilton Hotel. Sailing is an increasingly popular sport at which Israel is starting to compete at Olympic level. A number of marinas have been built or are in the process of construction. Tel-Aviv has a marina and so does Haifa, where the best sea-going yachts have been built. Herzlia municipality has decided to build one on its seafront.

Israel's sporting achievements may appear to be modest, but when the size of the population and the dramatic odds are taken into account, they are quite impressive. The emphasis is on sport as leisure not as competition, surely the most healthy attitude in the nature of modern society.

OPPOSITE LEFT *These water slides, called glitz-glatz in Hebrew, are a very popular innovation. This one is at the George Washington Sports Complex in Jerusalem; there is also one at the Sea of Galilee.*

OPPOSITE RIGHT *The beach at Herzliya, the resort north of Tel-Aviv where most of Israel's most elegant hotels are situated. Israel has miles and miles of sandy beaches. Breakwaters and other installations have made the often-dangerous Mediterranean coastline safe for bathing.*

ABOVE *Skiing on Mount Hermon. Organized skiing has only been possible since 1967, when all the slopes of Mount Hermon were conquered by Israel. It is quite possible in winter to ski in the morning in the mountain and swim in the Sea of Galilee in the afternoon.*

RIGHT *Scuba diving and windsurfing in the Red Sea. The beach at Eilat is covered with white, coarse sand created by the coral reefs.*

THE NEXT FORTY YEARS

LEFT This young Israeli holding a red pepper and a melon may not spend the rest of her life working on the land. As agriculture becomes more mechanized and large scale becomes important, even the farming settlements are becoming more deeply involved in industry, particularly high-tech industries.

'But Judah shall dwell forever and Jerusalem from
generation to generation.'

JOEL 3:20

IN THE FIRST 40 YEARS of its existence,
Israel has made the most spectacular progress, and
has actually become a world leader in certain
areas. Its achievements have been won against
overwhelming odds – the poverty of the land
resources, constant wars, the ever-present threat from its neighbours, mass immigration, much of it of people unfit for skilled
work for various reasons.

All this has not been achieved without cost. Israel has always
suffered from higher inflation than the European and North
American average. In the early 1980s, that inflation grew to world
record levels of three figures. Yet, miraculously, it was brought
under control with a minimum of political upheaval and today
the economy is largely back on course.

The coming of the computer age has been greatly to Israel's
advantage, for here is an industry that requires the minimum of
raw materials with the maximum of skill and innovative thinking.
Israel is likely to become ever more productive in this field, as in
other fields of technology. Already, 90 per cent of Israeli exports
are industrial; in 1948, this sector was virtually non-existent.

In 1948, there were 408,000 acres (165,250 hectares) of land
under cultivation. Today there are 1,067,000 acres (432,150 hectares); the value of agricultural produce has increased from

RIGHT *Construction of the Nahal
Hayun Dam. Israel's most vital resource
is water and the lack of it is a major
problem. Every available means to
gather water from the air, ground and
sea is being explored.*

LEFT *Science laboratory at the Hebrew
University's Givat Ram campus,
Jerusalem. Israel is a world leader in
some technical and scientific fields,
including the production of scanners for
medicine and computerized printing
equipment.*

RIGHT *A field of genetically improved
and adapted oregano at the Volcani
Institute, Israel's main agricultural
research station, in Rehovot. Israel's
scientific approach to agriculture has
enabled the country to increase exports of
fresh food at a time when it faces serious
competition from domestic markets in
Europe and North America.*

165

TOP RIGHT *The checkpoint sign at the Allenby Bridge, on the River Jordan, the only place where one can cross from Israel into Jordan. Israeli Arabs and those in the West Bank and Gaza may cross into Jordan but not Jews.*

ABOVE RIGHT *'Peace Now' anti-war demonstrators at a rally in Tel-Aviv to mark the first anniversary of the Israeli invasion of Lebanon. There are alleged to have been as many as 100,000 at the rally, protesting Israel's policy in Lebanon and demanding immediate withdrawal. That number is a sizable percentage of the Israeli Jewish population.*

U.S.$130 million in 1949 to U.S.$600 million today, a rise of 6 per cent per year, making it one of the fastest-growing agricultural economies in the world. In 1948, virtually all the agricultural exports were of citrus; today, a wide variety of tropical and sub-tropical fruit and vegetables is exported, as well as some fish and animal products. The export of flowers, made possible by better air transport, is becoming increasingly important.

Even here, there is room for expansion. The drip-feed irrigation technique is still relatively new, even in Israel where it was first developed, and more land could be brought under cultivation using this method.

Although Israel's population of four million might seem large for such a small country, there is still room for more – and there is always a home in Israel for Jews escaping persecution. Israel will never again have to face the influx which doubled the population between 1948 and 1952. The only large concentrations of Jews left outside Israel are in the United States, western Europe and the USSR. The Jews in the West are unlikely to be forced to seek shelter in large numbers, and the Jews of the Soviet Union, if they ever leave in large numbers, will not all come to Israel. In any case, these populations consist of highly educated and skilled people whose absorption would be of enormous benefit in both the short and long term.

The future is bright for Israel, but one thing would make it even brighter – peace with her neighbours. That will not come overnight; memories are long in the Middle East and even private feuds between families last for hundreds of years. Yet, despite serious intermittent setbacks, the signs are there. Between 1948 and 1967, there was absolutely no contact whatsover between Israel and her neighbours. Since 1967, people from all over the Arab world flock to Israel over the Allenby Bridge to visit relatives and friends or seek medical treatment, and in recent years Israeli Moslems have been permitted by the Saudi authorities to make the pilgrimage to Mecca. The gates are beginning to open, and the day draws nearer when Israel and the Arabs lay down their arms 'and study war no more'.

ALL ISRAEL

APPENDIX

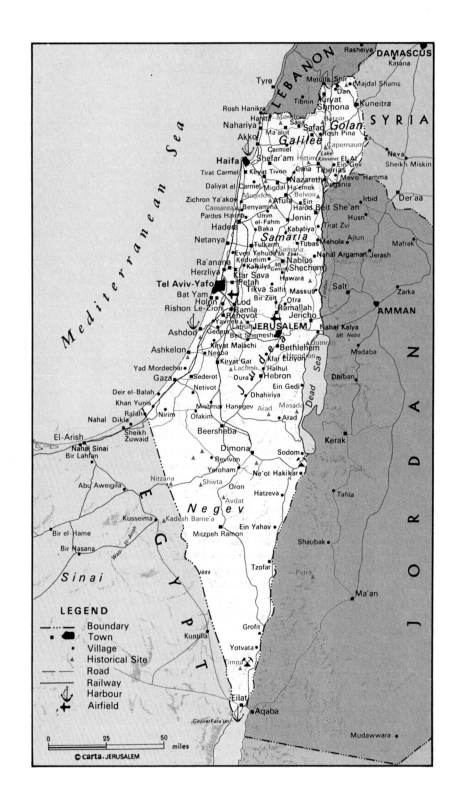

DAMASCUS
Rasheiya
Katana

Tyre
LEBANON
Metulla Snir
Majdal Shams
Dan
Kiryat
Shmona
Kuneitra

Rosh Hanikra
Hanita
SYRIA
Nahariya
Sasa
Golan
Nava
Akko
Ma'alot
Safad
Rosh Pina
Sheikh Miskin
Carmiel
Galilee
Haifa
Shefar'am
Capernaum
El Al
Tirat Carmel
Kiryat Tivon
Lake Kinneret
Ein Gev
Cana
Tiberias
Daliyat el Carmel
Migdal Ha'emek
Nazareth
Mevo Hamma
Zichron Ya'akov
Megiddo
Afula
Ein
Degania
Benyamina
Belvoir
Harod
Beit She'an
Irbid
Der'aa
Caesarea
Pardes Hanna
Umm
el-Fahm
Jenin
Husn
Hadera
Baka
Kabatiya
Tirat Zvi
Ajlun
Mafrak
Netanya
Samaria
Tubas
Mehola
Tulkarm
Nahal Argaman
Jerash
Even Yehuda
Samaria
Mt Ebal
Kedumim
Nablus
Zarka
Ra'anana
Kalkilya
Shechem
Herzliya
Mt
Gerizim
Hawara
Kfar Sava
Massua
Salt
Tel Aviv-Yafo
Petah
Tikva
Salfit
Bat Yam
Bir Zeit
Ofra
AMMAN
Holon
Lod
Ramallah
Jericho
Rishon Le-Zion
Rehovot
Ramla
Yavneh
Latrun
JERUSALEM
Nahal Kalya
Ashdod
Gedera
Mt Nebo
Beit Shemesh
Bethlehem
Ashkelon
Kiryat Malachi
Nebbe
Qumran
Madaba
Kiryat Gat
Kfar Etzion
Yad Mordechai
Lachish
Halhul
Dhiban
Gaza
Sederot
Dura
Hebron
Netivot
Deir el-Balah
Ein Gedi
Khan Yunis
Dhahiriya
Nahal Dikla
Rafah
Mishmar Hanegev
Masada
Nirim
Ofakim
Arad
Arad
El-Arish
Sheikh
Zuwaid
Beersheba
Kerak
Nahal Sinai
Bir Lahfan
Dimona
Sodom
Abu Aweigila
Nitzana
Revivim
Ne'ot Hakikar
Yeroham
Bir el-Hame
Kusseima
Shivta
Oron
Hatzeva
Tafila
Bir Nasana
Avdat
Negev
Kadesh Barne'a
Ein Yahav
Mitzpeh Ramon
Shaubak
Sinai
Tzofar
Petra
Ma'an
Grofit
Kuntilla
Yotvata
Timna
EGYPT
JORDAN
Eilat
Aqaba
Geziret Fara'un
Mudawwara

Mediterranean Sea

Dead Sea

Judea

LEGEND
- ▪ Boundary
- ■ Town
- • Village
- ▲ Historical Site
- — Road
- — Railway
- ⚓ Harbour
- ✈ Airfield

0   25   50 miles

© carta, JERUSALEM

· BIBLIOGRAPHY ·

The number of books about the history of Israel, Zionism and the Middle East are legion. The best known and most popular is, of course, the Bible.

ALLBRIGHT, William, *The Archaeology of Palestine* (London: Penguin Books, 1960)

BAKER, H E, *The Legal System of Israel* (Jerusalem, 1968)

BARGAD, Warren and CHYET, Stanley, *Israeli Poetry* (Bloomington: Indiana University Press, 1986)

BEN-GURION, David, *Israel, A Personal History* (New York: Funk & Wagnalls, 1971)

BEN-SASSON, Haim H (Ed), *A History of the Jewish People* (Cambridge, Mass: Harvard University Press, 1976)

CARMI, T (Ed), *The Penguin Book of Hebrew Verse* (London: Penguin Books, 1982)

CHURCHILL, Randolph and Winston, *The Six-Day War* (London: Heinemann, 1967)

EBAN, Abba, *My People, The Story of the Jews* (New York: Behrman House, Inc, 1968)

IBID, *Heritage: Civilization and the Jews* (London: Weidenfeld and Nicolson, 1984)

Encyclopaedia Judaica, 16 vols (Jerusalem: Keter Publishing, 1972)

Encyclopedia of Israel and Zionism, 2 vols (New York: McGraw-Hill, 1971)

Facts about Israel (Jerusalem: Ministry of Foreign Affairs, 1985)

HALKIN, Simon, *Modern Hebrew Literature: From the Enlightenment to the Birth of the State of Israel* (New York: Schocken Books, 1970)

HERZL, Theodor, *Old-New Land* (trans L Levensohn), (New York, 1960)

HERZOG, Chaim and GIHON, Mordechai, *Battles of the Bible* (London: Weidenfeld and Nicolson, 1979)

KUTSCHER, E Y, *A History of the Hebrew Language* (Jerusalem and Leiden, 1982)

LAQUEUR, Walter, *A History of Zionism* (London: Weidenfeld and Nicolson, 1972)

PRITTIE, Terence, *Israel: Miracle in the Desert* (London: Pall Mall, 1967)

SACHAR, Howard M, *A History of Israel, from the Rise of Zionism to Our Time* (Oxford: Basil Blackwell, 1977)

SMOOHA, Sammy and CIBULSKI, Ora, *Social Research on Arabs in Israel, 1948–1977, Trends and Annotated Bibliography* (Ramat Gan: Turtledove Publishing, 1978)

SPICEHANDLER, Ezra (Ed), *New Writing in Israel* (New York: Schocken Books, 1976)

SYKES, Christopher, *Crossroads to Israel* (London: Collins, 1965)

VITAL, David, *Zionism: The Formative Years* (London: Oxford University Press, 1982)

WEIZMANN, Chaim, *Trial and Error: The Autobiography of Chaim Weizmann* (New York: Harper and Row, 1965)

YANUN, Avraham, *Some Focal Topics in the Literature of the Arabs of Israel*, Hamizrah He-Hadash (Jerusalem, 1965)

IBID, *Social Topics in the Literature in the Arabs of Israel* (Jerusalem, 1966)

YUDKIN, Leon, *Escape into Siege* (London: Oxford University Press, 1974)

'1948 AND AFTER: ASPECTS OF ISRAELI FICTION' (Manchester: Journal of Semitic Studies, Monograph Series, 1984)

ZANDER, W, *Israel and the Holy Places of Christendom*, (London, 1971)

• SOURCES •

TOURIST OFFICES, EMBASSIES AND RELATED ORGANIZATIONS

ISRAEL
Israel Government Tourist Office
24 King George St
Jerusalem
Tel: (02) 23 73 11

Israel Automobile and Touring Club
Head Office
19 Petah Tikvah Rd
Tel-Aviv
Tel: (03) 62 29 61 or 62

There are also branches in Beer-Sheba, Haifa, Jerusalem, Netanya and Tiberias.

UK
Israel Government Tourist Office
18 Great Marlborough St
London W1V 1AF
Tel: (01) 434 3651

Embassy of Israel
2 Palace Green
London W8
Tel: (01) 937 8050

El Al Israel Airlines
185 Regent St
London W1
Tel: (01) 437 9255

USA
Israel Government Tourist Office
350 Fifth Ave
New York, NY 10018
Tel: (212) 560 0650

Israel Government Tourist Office
5 South Wabash Ave
Chicago, IL 60603
Tel: (312) 782 4306

Israel Government Tourist Office
6380 Wilshire Blvd
Los Angeles, CA 90048
Tel: (213) 658 7462

Israel Government Tourist Office
4151 Southwest Freeway
Houston, TX 77027
Tel: (713) 850 9341

Embassy of Israel
3514 International Drive
Washingtion, DC 20008
Tel: (202) 364 5500

El Al Israel Airlines
Rockefeller Center
16 W 49th St
New York, NY 10020
Tel: 1-800 223 6700 (toll free)

CANADA
Israel Government Tourist Office
102 Bloor Street West
Toronto, Ont M5S 1M8
Tel: (416) 964 3784

Embassy of Israel
410 Laurier Ave West
Ottawa, Ont K1R 7T3

SELECTED TOUR OPERATORS TO ISRAEL
(most include travel for the disabled)

UK
Israel Air, Tour Operators
Triumph House
189 Regent St
London W1
Tel: (01) 437 2892

USA
Arkia Israeli Airlines
350 Fifth Ave
New York, NY 10018
Tel: (212) 695 2998

Avantours
8500 Wilshire Blvd
Beverly Hills, CA 90211
Tel: (213) 652 2160

Bible Land Travel
1204 E Main St
Smithtown, NY 11787
Tel: (502) 636 9211

Catholic Travel Office
1019 19th St, NW, Suite 520
Washington, DC 20036
Tel: (202) 293 2277

Command Travel
6 E 45th St
New York, NY 10017
Tel: (212) 490 1213

Concorde 55 Israel Ltd
56 W 45th St
New York, NY 10036
Tel: (212) 391-8681

Council on International Educational Exchange
205 E 42nd St
New York, NY 10017
Tel: (212) 661 0311

Kopel Tours Ltd
40 E 49th St
New York, NY 10017
Tel: (212) 838-0500

BUSINESSES AND BUSINESS ORGANIZATIONS

UK
British-Israel Chamber of Commerce
Information and Trade Centre
126-134 Baker St
London W1M 1FH
Tel: (01) 486 2371

Bank Leumi (UK) plc
4/7 Woodstock St (main office)
London W1A 2AF
Tel: (01) 629 1205

Carmel Wine Company Ltd
Palwin House
7–9 Club Row
London E1
Tel: (01) 739 4771

USA
American-Israel Chamber of Commerce
and Industry
500 Fifth Ave
New York, NY 10017
Tel: (212) 354 6510
Branches in major American cities

P.E.C. Israel Economic Corp
511 Fifth Ave
New York, NY 10017

LIBRARIES, GALLERIES, MUSEUMS AND RELATED SOCIETIES

UK
Anglo-Israel Archaeological Society
3 St John's Wood Rd
London NW8
Tel: (01) 286 1176

Ben Uri Art Gallery
21 Dean St
London W1
Tel: (01) 437 2852

British Israel Numismatic Assn
Hon. Sec: L C Goss

42 Golders Green
London NW11 9BU
Tel: (01) 455 5599

Jewish Museum
Woburn House
Upper Woburn Place
London WC1 0EP
Tel: (01) 388 4525
Hours: Sun (& Fri during winter), 10am–
12.45pm; Tues to Thurs (& Fri during
summer), 10am–4pm. Closed Mon, Sat,
public & Jewish holidays.

USA
Jewish Museum
1109 Fifth Ave, at 92nd St
New York, NY 10028
Hours: Mon to Thurs, 12–5pm; Sun, 11–6.

Yeshiva University Museum
2520 Amsterdam Ave, at 185th St
New York, NY 10033
Hours: Tues–Thurs, 11–5; Sun, 12–6; or by
appt, (212) 960 5390

Maurice Spertus Museum of Judaica
618 S Michigan Ave
Chicago, IL
Hours: Mon to Thurs, 10–5; Fri &
Sun, 10–3.

B'nai B'rith Museum
1640 Rhode Island Ave
Washington, DC
Hours: Sun-Fri, 10–5

Museum of Jewish History
55 N 5th St

Independence Mall East
Philadelphia, PA
Hours: Sun to Thurs, 10–5; Fri, 1-4.

Hebrew Union College Skirball
Museum
3077 University Mall
Los Angeles, CA
Hours: Tues to Fri, 11–4; Sun, 10–5.

EDUCATIONAL AND CULTURAL INSTITUTIONS, AFFILIATED ORGANIZATIONS

UK
Friends of the Hebrew University
of Jerusalem
3 St John's Wood
London NW8 8RB
Tel: (01) 286 1176

British Technion Society
83 Wimpole St
London W1M 7DB
Tel: (01) 486 0356

USA
American Associates of
Ben-Gurion University of Negev
342 Madison Ave, Rm 1923
New York, NY 10017

American Committee for
Weizmann Institute
515 Park Ave
New York, NY 10022

American Friends of Haifa University
206 Fifth Ave, 4th floor
New York, NY 10010

American Friends of the Hebrew
University
11 E 69th St
New York, NY 10021

American Friends of Tel-Aviv University
342 Madison Ave
New York, NY 10017

American Technion Society
271 Madison Ave
New York, NY 10016

Bar-Ilan University in Israel
527 Madison Ave
New York, NY 10022

Jewish Theological Seminary
3080 Broadway
New York, NY 10027

National Foundation for Jewish Culture
1512 Chanin Building
122 E 42nd St
New York, NY 10168

ZIONIST ORGANIZATIONS,

including those involved in arranging volunteers to work in Israel on kibbutzim

UK

Zionist Federation of Great Britain and Northern Ireland
Balfour House
741 High Rd
London N12 0BQ
Tel: (01) 446 1477

Youth and Hehalutz Dept
World Zionist Organization
Balfour House
741 High Rd
London N12 0BQ
Tel: (01) 446 1477

The Balfour Diamond Jubilee Trust
40 Portland Place
London W1
British Aliya Movement
Balfour House
741 High Rd
London N12 0BQ
Tel: (01) 446 1477

USA

American Jewish League for Israel
30 E 60th St
New York, NY 10022

American Zionist Federation
515 Park Ave
New York, NY 10022

American Zionist Youth Foundation
515 Park Ave
New York, NY 10022

Hadassah Women's Zionist
Organization of America
50 W 58th St
New York, NY 10019

Theodor Herzl Foundation
515 Park Ave
New York, NY 10022

Jewish National Fund
42 E 69th St
New York, NY 10021

World Zionist Organization
4 E 34th St
New York, NY 10016

CANADA

Canadian Zionist Federation
1310 Greene Ave
Montreal, Que

Canadian Zionist Federation
111 Finch Ave West
Downsview, Ont

Zionist Organization of Canada
788 Marlee Ave
Toronto, Ont

AUSTRALIA

Zionist Federation of Australia
146 Darlinghurst Rd
Darlinghurst, NSW 2010

NEW ZEALAND

New Zealand Zionist Federation
PO Box 4315
Auckland

SOUTH AFRICA

South African Zionist Federation
PO Box 18
Johannesburg 20000

OTHER

UK

Anglo-Israel Association
9 Bentinck St
London W1
Tel: (01) 486 2300

Friends of Israel Association
741 High Rd
Finchley
London N12 0BQ
Tel: (01) 446 1477

USA

American-Israel Cultural Foundation
485 Madison Ave
New York, NY 10022

American-Israel Public Affairs
Committee
444 N Capitol St, NW, Suite 412
Washington, DC 20001

INDEX

175

• PICTURE CREDITS •

THE PUBLISHERS have made every effort to identify the copyright holders of the photographs used in this book; they apologize for any omissions and would like to thank the following:

Key: *l*=left; *r*=right; *t*=top; *b*=bottom; *c*=centre; *m*=main picture; *i*=inset picture.

ALL-SPORT (UK) LTD: pages 157 (photo. Chris Cole), 158 *t* (All Sport/Vandystadt), 158 *b*, 159 (Bob Martin). ASSOCIATED PRESS: pages 44, 71 *t*, 80/1, 96 *t*, 97, 165. JOSEPHINE BACON: pages 39 *bl*, 72 *t*, 87 *t*, 109 *tr*, 155 *tr*. BAT-DOR DANCE COMPANY: page 140. BET HATEFUTZOT (The Nahum Goldmann Museum of the Jewish Diaspora): pages 84 *r*, 85. DOROTHY BOHM: pages 70, 71 *b*, 134 *t*. BRITISH-ISRAEL PUBLIC AFFAIRS COMMITTEE: pages 12 *bl*, 16 (Klaus Otto Hundt), 17 *l*, 17 *tr* (Klaus Otto Hundt), 20 *t* (Klaus Otto Hundt), 20 *b*, 21 *r*, 22, 23 *bl*, 24 *tl*, 24 *bl* (Ronald Dean), 25, 26 (Klaus Otto Hundt), 27 *l* (Klaus Otto Hundt), 27 *r*, 28, 29 (Frank D Smith), 31-2 (Klaus Otto Hundt), 33 *l tr* (Adam Greene), 33 *br*, 34, 35 *r*, 38 *l*, 38 *r* (D White), 39 *r*, 40 (D Dean), 41-3, 46, 47 *t* (D White), 47 *b*, 48, 50, 52 (Klaus Otto Hundt), 53-4 (Netta Saraph), 55-6, 58-9, 60 *l*, 61 (Adam Greene), 64, 66/7, 68 (Frank D Smith), 69 *l*, 72 *b* (D White), 73 *l tr*, 74 (Simon Lewis), 75, 80 *t*, 83, 84 *l* (D White), 88, 89 *t* (Klaus Otto Hundt), 90-4, 95 *t*, 96 *c b*, 98, 100-3, 105, 113-4, 120/1 (Klaus Otto Hundt), 122 *l tr*, 123 (Simon Lewis), 124 *t br* (Klaus Otto Hundt), 124 *bl* (Frank Smith), 127 *l* (Adam Greene), 128 *m* (Klaus Otto Hundt), 128 *i* (Adam Greene), 129 *tr* (Klaus Otto Hundt), 129 *br*, 129 *bl* (Simon Lewis), 130 *br* (Klaus Otto Hundt), 132, 135 *tl*, 146, 148 *b*, 150 (Netta Saraph), 151 *tr*, 154 *t*, 156, 160 *b*, 161, 164 *br*. BRITISH TECHNION SOCIETY: pages 116, 118. CHATTO AND WINDUS, LONDON: page 117 *l*. DE BEERS CONSOLIDATED MINES: page 122 *br*. BRETZ-ISRAEL MUSEUM: pages 135 *tr*, 136 *l*. FRIENDS OF THE HEBREW UNIVERSITY, JERUSALEM: pages 12 *r*, 76, 99, 125, 126 *r*, 135 *bl*, 164 *bl*. HAIFA MUNICIPAL THEATRE, ISRAEL (photo. M. Derfler): page 142. ISRAEL FILM ARCHIVES: page 143. ISRAEL MUSEUM, JERUSALEM: pages 36, 78 *b* (Collection of Israel Dept. of Antiquities), 79 (Collection of Israel Dept. of Antiquities), 82 *t* (Collection of The Shrine of the Book), 82 *b* (Collection of Israel Dept. of Antiquities, photo. IM/David Harris), 110 *tr* (Collection of Israel Dept. of Antiquities, photo. IM/David Harris), 110 *br* (Collection of The Shrine of the Book), 136 *r* (photo. IM/David Harris), 137 *l tr* (photo. IM/David Harris), 137 *br* (Collection of the artist, photo. IM/Moshe Caine), 138 *bl* (photo. Reuven Milon), 138 *tl r*, 139. ISRAELI TOURIST BOARD, NEW YORK: pages 6, 8, 18/19, 49, 60 *r*, 62-3, 66, 109 *b*, 129 *cr*, 148 *t*, 152-3, 155 *l br*. JEWISH NATIONAL FUND: pages 10, 12 *tl*, 18, 57, 127 *r*, 131, 160 *l*, 162, 164/5. THE JEWISH QUARTERLY ARCHIVE: page 115. DANI LANDAU: pages 106, 108, 144, 154 *b*. ZIGALIT LANDAU: page 134 *b*. THE MINISTRY OF COMMUNICATIONS, ISRAEL: pages 35 *l*, 104, 110 *l*, 112, 130 *t*. WALTER NELSON & ASSOCIATES: page 130 *bl*. PALPHOT LTD, ISRAEL: pages 17 *br*, 23 *t br*. QUARTO PUBLISHING PLC (photo. Ian Howes): pages 9, 10/11, 13, 14, 21 *l*, 24 *r*, 30/1, 37, 39 *tl*, 69 *r*, 73 *br*, 78 *t*, 80 *b*, 86, 87 *b*, 89 *b*, 95 *b*, 149, 151 *tl bl*. ZED BOOKS, LONDON: page 117 *r*.